E242
EDUCATION: A SECOND-LEVEL COURSE

LEARNING FOR ALL

UNIT 13
FURTHER AND HIGHER

Prepared for the course team by
Janice Wearmouth, Elizabeth Maudslay and Bernadette McAnespie
with contributions from Jenny Corbett

The Open University

E242 COURSE READERS

There are two course readers associated with E242; they are:
BOOTH, T., SWANN, W., MASTERTON, M. and POTTS, P. (eds) (1992) *Learning for All 1: curricula for diversity in education*, London, Routledge/The Open University (**Reader 1**).

BOOTH, T., SWANN, W., MASTERTON, M. and POTTS, P. (eds) (1992) *Learning for All 2: policies for diversity in education*, London, Routledge/The Open University (**Reader 2**).

TELEVISION PROGRAMMES AND AUDIO-CASSETTES

There are seven TV programmes and two audio-cassettes associated with E242. They are closely integrated into the unit texts and there are no separate TV or cassette notes. However, further information about them may be obtained by writing to Open University Educational Enterprises Ltd, 12 Cofferidge Close, Stony Stratford, Milton Keynes MK11 1BY.

AUTHORS' ACKNOWLEDGEMENT

The authors would like to thank Tony Booth, Jenny Corbett and Sally Tomlinson for their contributions to the development of this text.

Cover illustration shows a detail from *Midsummer Common* by Dorothy Bordass.

The Open University, Walton Hall, Milton Keynes MK7 6AA

First published 1992. This edition published 1997. Reprinted 1998

Copyright © 1997 The Open University

All rights reserved. No part of this publication may be reproduced, stored in a retrieval system or transmitted, in any form or by any means, without either the prior written permission from the publisher or a licence permitting restricted copying issued by the Copyright Licensing Agency Limited, 90 Tottenham Court Road, London W1P 9HE. This book may not be lent, resold, hired out or otherwise disposed of by way of trade in any form of binding or cover other than that in which it is published, without the prior consent of the publisher.

Edited, designed and typeset by The Open University.

Printed in the United Kingdom by Page Bros, Norwich.

ISBN 0 7492 7581 2

This unit forms part of an Open University course; the complete list of units is printed at the end of this book. If you have not enrolled on the course and would like to buy this or other Open University material, please write to Open University Educational Enterprises Ltd, The Open University, Walton Hall, Milton Keynes, MK7 6AA. If you wish to enquire about enrolling as an Open University student, please write to the Courses Reservations and Sales Centre, The Open University, PO Box 724, Walton Hall, Milton Keynes MK7 6ZS, United Kingdom.

CONTENTS

1	**Introduction**	5
2	**Transition**	6
	Perspectives on transition	7
	The transition process in education: advice contained in the Code of Practice	16
	Summary	17
3	**Further education**	18
	The development of further education	18
	A historical perspective	18
	The move to vocationalism	22
	Funding further education	25
	Centralized funding	25
	Local funding	26
	Implications of variation in funding	26
	Limitations of the FEFC system of funding	27
	Support and participation	30
	The range of provision	31
	Link courses	35
	Evaluating further education	36
	Students' views	36
	The Tomlinson review	40
	Notions of inclusion	42
	Summary	44
4	**Training and employment**	45
	Training and Enterprise Councils	45
	Social services	48
	Local authority provision: adult education	48
	Training and employment schemes	48
	Case study – the 'Unlocking Employment' project	49
	Access to employment	52
	Summary	53

5	**Higher education**	53
	Widening access	53
	Summary	57
6	**Conclusion**	57
	Equality of opportunity for all?	57
7	**Investigations**	60
	Views on inclusion	60
	Policy for equal opportunities	60
	Transition in the Code of Practice	61
	Appendix 1 The transition section in the Code of Practice	62
	Appendix 2 The organization of 'additional support' provision in FE colleges	70
	Appendix 3 Beyond the 'inclusionist' debate	75
	References	79
	Acknowledgements	80

1 INTRODUCTION

1.1   This unit has two main themes: transition from adolescence to adulthood, and the issue of inclusion in relation to young people and adults in further, higher and adult education, and on courses related to training and employment. Everyone's choices are constrained by political and economic factors, by regional variations in the pattern of opportunities and, for many, by discrimination on the basis of their disability, race, gender or class. We examine the progress made in recent years towards increasing participation, reducing barriers and promoting equality of opportunity. We explore who is being included and excluded from education, training and employment, and what young people and adults have to say about what they would like for themselves. We ask you to reflect on how you think a civilized society should respond to the educational and training needs of all young people and adults, including those who are marginalized socially, economically and occupationally, and to consider how resources could be harnessed to enable everyone to live a personally fulfilling life.

1.2   In the first section (Section 2) we examine the concept of transition from adolescence to adulthood and the complex notion of 'adult status'. We then look at the practicalities of the transition process as defined in the *Code of Practice on the Identification and Assessment Of Special Educational Needs*.

1.3   In Section 3 we give a brief overview of further education, looking at how it differs from compulsory schooling, the variety of ways in which it is funded, and how this funding determines the level of provision and support. We also explore the current debate around integration and inclusion in further education, include case studies which exemplify different approaches to making provision for all students, and discuss the Tomlinson Report which evaluated provision in further education for students who experience difficulties in learning and/or who have disabilities.

1.4   In Section 4 we examine training and employment, offer examples of options which may be available, and indicate some of the constraints on opportunity.

1.5   In Section 5 we look at opportunities for students in higher education, showing how they vary in relation to the age and history of each institution and discuss recent initiatives designed to widen access.

1.6   In Section 6, we conclude by asking you to reflect on how far you feel there is equality of opportunity for everyone in further and higher education and on schemes related to employment, what action you consider should be taken, and how you feel the current situation reflects the value placed on individuals in our society.

HOW TO STUDY THIS UNIT

1.7 In addition to the main text you will be asked to read the following material:

Section 2 Transition

Reader 2, Chapter 10: 'An international perspective on transition' by John Fish.

Reader 2, Chapter 11: 'The rhetoric and reality of transition to adult life' by Jenny Corbett and Len Barton.

Appendix 1: The transition section of the Code of Practice.

Section 3 Further education

Reader 2, Chapter 12: 'Supporting special needs in further education' by Maureen Turnham.

Appendix 2: Provision in two colleges.

Reader 1, Chapter 6: 'Setting the agenda: student participation on a multi-media learning scheme' by Stuart Olesker.

Appendix 3: Beyond the 'inclusionist' debate.

Section 4 Training and employment

Reader 1, Chapter 21: 'From school to schemes: out of education into training' by Robert Holland.

2 TRANSITION

2.1 Important changes occur in people's lives as they move from childhood to adulthood. In education, the age of 16 is important because it marks a transition from the statutory to the non-statutory sector. Most students continue with their education in one form or another beyond that age. The percentage continuing in full-time education at 17 has risen from 10 per cent in 1955 to 59 per cent in 1994/5. The percentage of 18–19 year olds proceeding into higher education has risen from 4 per cent in 1955 to 31 per cent in 1994/5. For many students making decisions about training or education, there are well defined pathways to follow, for example moving on into a school sixth form or a local college to follow A-level courses or a vocational programme. However, for a significant minority of students who have already experienced considerable difficulties in the education system, the progression may be far less clear.

2.2 In this section we ask you first to reflect on your own ideas about adolescence and adulthood. We then look at some of the difficulties which may arise where there is a mismatch between the student's wants and needs and what is available and provide examples of how other countries have attempted to overcome these difficulties. Finally, we discuss the transition process in education prescribed by the *Code of Practice for the Identification and Assessment of Special Educational Needs*.

PERSPECTIVES ON TRANSITION

Activity 1 Transition to adult life

What does 'adolescence' mean to you? What does 'adulthood' mean to you? What might make it difficult for young people who experience difficulties in learning, who have been disaffected from the school system, or who have disabilities, to make the transition to adolescence and adulthood?

Read the following descriptions of four people's everyday lives and consider:

- What options did Peter, Christine, Mark and Rosalee have to secure a way of life that suits them?

- Would you say they are leading 'adult' lives?

Peter

Peter is now 21. He was a student at a special school, and went from there to a special two-year college course and then on to a Youth Training programme. In some areas of the country he would have been guided towards the social education centre and sheltered employment. Instead, he is supported in a work placement for four days a week in the kitchen of a local hotel. He spends the fifth day on a college catering course. In the hotel kitchen he prepares vegetables, washes up and bakes cakes and biscuits. Peter was sacked from two previous work placements for his lack of concentration and unpredictability. Without the active and sustained support of the programme's staff and his sympathetic new employers, Peter would not have the degree of control over his life that he now enjoys. He hopes to continue working in the hotel when his training period is completed.

Peter has recently moved out of his parents' home into a house which he shares with two other young men. They have daily support and are expected to share household chores. Peter is an active member of the village community in which he lives, for example taking part in the musicals which are sometimes presented.

However, Peter still visits his parents every weekend and wants their regular help and guidance. It is also true that sometimes Peter does not want to participate in the social life of his new home nor to co-operate at work. Like most people, Peter feels more ready to accept responsibilities on some days than on others.

Christine

Christine is 22, dyslexic, and has a temporary post as a classroom assistant in a school for pupils with severe physical disabilities. She was about 11 when she realized she was finding reading and spelling more difficult than some other pupils. When the teacher had time she used to take her out of the class for individual tuition, but Christine never knew when that was going to happen so she missed parts of other lessons and felt she was always behind her peers. She recalls other students saying cruel things to her, such as 'Oh, she's thick, she's stupid. She doesn't know what she's doing.' Christine did know what she was doing, but trying to write it down on paper was impossible for her.

By the age of 13 she had given up on school and on teachers. Everyone seemed to be against her, whatever she was doing, and in the end she remembers, 'I mucked around to get a bit of attention. I never did any homework. I got into trouble, but I just gave up and they gave up. They just put me in the group of other kids who just mucked around. Obviously, you've always got people in the class who want to muck around. You're blaming the teacher, so if you can wind them up you do.' She used to write all over the tables because they hated it. She would amuse herself by calling the teachers' names out loud in class. 'Whatever you could do to disrupt the class, you'd do it. The French teacher used to go out of the class, so we'd get hairspray and set light to it as it sprayed out. One French lesson, my friend got this little bottle of gin and we just sat there drinking it under the table.'

Christine did not do well in her GCSE exams. She had no intention of doing any revision because she had nothing to revise from. After she had taken notes, often as dictation from the teacher, she couldn't understand what she had written.

She left school at 16, interested in pursuing a career in nursery nursing. Subsequently she took a one year college course in childcare designed for students with 'learning difficulties', and then a series of temporary jobs as a nanny, with spells of unemployment in between. At the age of 19 she was offered a further full-time two-year college course in nursery nursing. At the time she was employed and was advised by her parents and her employer to turn down the offer because it would entail the potential loss of earnings for two years, with no guarantee of a job at the end of the course. She followed their advice, but afterward deeply regretted it.

Christine is now determined to do something about what she sees as lost opportunities and find a way to become fully qualified as a nursery nurse.

Mark

Mark is a prison inmate. When he was a child, his father used to sit in front of the television all day long, drinking and smoking. He recollects that all he wanted at that time was to have a normal father going to work every day with a briefcase in his hand, like the other children had. His father used to beat him, and his mother eventually got a divorce.

There was a lot of instability for Mark after his parents separated and he was sent to a children's home when he was 12. It was a terrible shock to his system. He recalls the behaviour in the home being 'wild'. Some of the children once made Molotov cocktails, set fire to them and threw them against the wall of the building. Every day he went from one context in which there appeared to him to be no control at all to another which was tightly controlled and where he was expected to sit silently in a row and listen. He felt he was becoming schizophrenic. 'School was totally out of it as far as I was concerned,' he now says.

In the secondary schools he attended, the punishment for not handing in homework on time was a detention after school. Mark used to refuse to do it. He recollects that nobody ever asked him *why* he hadn't done the homework. They just used to tell him off and humiliate him in front of the whole class. He says now, 'In a mixed ability group, when you spend the whole week with the same group, you have to live with this, with them seeing you humiliated in public. There are a lot of spiteful children in schools who will try and take it out of you.' Often he couldn't take pressure in class from the teachers and used to rush out to avoid tears in front of the others.

He spent one and a half years in his first secondary school before he was permanently excluded. He subsequently attended four more and left the last one when he was only 15. The teachers told him in his first year of secondary school that he was 'university material', but he was under a lot of pressure outside school, being sent from one home to another, and he was excluded from school after school, five in all. He remembers that at meetings teachers used to say things in front of him such as 'He is intelligent and has potential, but he also has behavioural problems. Considering he's a problem child, he's good at computers,' but nobody ever asked him what he thought about it. The first time he saw an educational psychologist she made him so angry that he went away and got hold of some books on child psychology so he could see where she was coming from. She couldn't get through to him at all after that because he put up so many barriers against her.

By the age of 14 he was truanting regularly. Once he earned £45 in cash per week helping to lay electric cables for someone. 'He know we were under age, even though we told him we were 16.'

On his sixteenth birthday Mark was given a bedsit to live in and a small allowance. He feels now that he had very little real support from anyone at that stage, and soon ran into debt with the landlord and lost his accommodation. He started living rough on the streets but, even so, tried at one point attending college. However, he could not keep himself clean enough not to be offensive to other students. He began stealing food for himself, and then other larger, more valuable items. He is now serving a prison sentence for these crimes.

Rosalee

Rosalee is now in her mid-thirties and a practising speech therapist. She was an only child and born blind. Her recollection of her childhood is that her parents felt uncomfortable in her presence as a result of her visual difficulty and sent her away to a boarding school for the blind where she spent the first six years of her school life. At the boarding school pupils were often afraid of the staff, and as a result of this fear a child had to have the tip of her finger amputated . She had wound an elastic band around it to stop it bleeding rather than ask for a sticking plaster, and after a day or so it had turned black and was beginning to develop gangrene.

After several operations on her eyes, Rosalee gained some sight, but her parents continued to send her away to school. This time it was a non-specialist school for girls. There Rosalee developed an ability to make lasting friendships, but not the ability to look after herself in a practical way. Her skill in making friends stood her in good stead when she later went to university to study English and realized she was going blind again. While she was a student there was no special provision for those with visual impairments, and she taught herself Braille. Her friends read her the texts that had not been printed in Braille. They also tried to teach her how to cook, but she always considered herself very impractical and was resistant to the idea. She preferred to work out other strategies for coping with practical difficulties other than those which would demand skills with her hands.

On leaving university the idea of going to live at home did not cross her mind. Instead, she found support from a charitable foundation to live independently in London and train as a speech therapist. There were occasions when she found herself in serious physical danger as she used public transport to travel alone through the city. One day she fell off the platform on to the line at a tube station, but was rescued by a stranger, with no regard for his own safety.

Rosalee continues to live alone, but has a wide but close circle of friends.

2.3 The period of adolescence is often linked to the idea of individuals gaining more personal autonomy, the opportunity to make decisions for themselves and developing the ability to take responsibility for the consequences of those decisions. Choices for Peter and Christine included continuing to live with parents or moving into alternative accommodation, taking 'dead-end' jobs or choosing training, attending college courses for students who experience difficulties in learning or moving into mainstream courses. When Mark and Rosalee left full-time education, however, their situation was different. They had to try to manage their own lives without assistance from their families. Mark had little support and no real opportunity for further education or employment. He also had to accept the consequences for all his own actions with no one to help him out when he ran into trouble. Unable to handle this unaccustomed autonomy, he soon lost his freedom altogether. Rosalee's family might have become over-protective because she was blind and might never have allowed her out alone in case she encountered the kind of danger that she did in fact face when she travelled around. Rosalee thought that her parents had never really seemed accept her visual impairment and had always kept her at a distance, and almost forced autonomy on her. Choice for her has been broadened through access to higher education and the status of 'professional'. However, it is limited by the fact that much of the necessary support for her everyday living continues to be provided through a charity and not as of right.

2.4   As we can see from the descriptions of the lives of these people, how people view adolescence and the needs of adolescents is not straightforward and varies within and between families, as well as culturally. The issue of personal autonomy is important to any young person but may be particularly significant for those who experience difficulties in learning, who have been disaffected from the school system, or who have disabilities. This is apparent in many aspects of these young people's lives, for example:

- Young people who experience difficulties in learning may be in a situation where they are rarely left alone and therefore do not have the privacy to develop personal relationships in a way that most adolescents enjoy, and are often denied the chance to live away from their family home. There may be a professional overseeing the individual's performance, hence that person may also be denied the chance to experiment, break rules, take risks and make mistakes, all of which form a usual part of many people's pathway into adolescence and adulthood. In many areas of the country, Peter would have been supervised. However, he lives in an area of the country where encouraging personal autonomy is seen by social services as important for everyone, and both his accommodation and his work placement reflect this.

- Where school discipline in the classroom depends on unquestioning compliance by students, the use of exclusion for 'disruptive' students is one means by which teachers can exercise control over a section of the school-student population perceived to demand too much autonomy and to be challenging to the social order. Exclusion usually results in restricted further education, training and employment opportunities. Mark has now been excluded from society altogether and removed to an institution where any choice for the inmates is almost entirely denied.

- Choice of employment-related training and/or further education course is very limited for those who leave school with few qualifications. This is a particularly frustrating situation for those who had the potential to gain qualifications relevant to their chosen career but were prevented from doing so by barriers to their learning. Christine now knows that dyslexia impeded her progress in school. She has yet to work out how she can gain the qualifications she needs and earn her own living at the same time.

- Young people with physical disabilities and sensory impairments are often denied the physical access which would allow them to socialize with their peers independently. Rosalee found travel difficult, especially because she had to rely on public transport and a white stick to alert other people to the fact that she might need assistance, but she persisted in her attempts to live as independently as possible, albeit with the support of a charitable agency.

2.5 The idea of transition to an adult life is complex and contradictory. Transition into employment is often cited as *the* important indicator of adult status, but there are difficulties with this view, especially when many young people cannot get jobs. In addition, employment may not be an appropriate activity for some adults, but this does not imply that they should be denied the dignity of being regarded as adult. A number of other factors has also been associated with the idea of what it means to be 'adult', for example personal independence, social interaction, the ability to adopt family roles (CERI, 1986), and living outside the family (Ward *et al.*, 1991).

Activity 2   Obstacles in transition

Now read 'An international perspective on transition' by John Fish (Reader 2, Chapter 10).

As you read, consider the following questions:

- How does John Fish define 'transition' and what it means to be an 'adult'?

- How far does his definition of adulthood reflect that of the wider society?

- What reasons does he give for the increased attention paid to the transition of young people who experience difficulties in learning, or who have disabilities, as they leave school and go on to further education, training and employment, unemployment or community living?

- What strategies does John Fish outline for making transitional practice easier and what examples of good practice does he give?

- What obstacles does he describe and how do you think these might be overcome?

2.6 John Fish supports a view of transition as both 'a phase and a process', involving moving from childhood, adolescence and dependence to an adulthood characterized by independence and wage-earning. These characteristics reflect accepted landmarks of change and maturity within a traditional Western culture but the extent to which they can be applied to all sections of the community is questionable. For example, does employment retain its importance as an indicator of adult status among groups, such as 18–25 year olds from ethnic minorities who have experienced disproportionately high levels of unemployment for many years? Fish acknowledges that there can be contradictions and that an individual's experience of transition can be confused.

2.7 For Fish the transition from adolescence to adulthood is one of the most important changes in our lives, and is especially important for young people with disabilities or learning difficulties. He suggests that demographic changes could result in improved job prospects for disadvantaged groups because there will be more jobs to go round. However, high youth unemployment and strong competition for vacancies remain. There is also evidence to suggest that changes in the types of jobs which are available (for example, greater emphasis on transferable skills and new technology) and the patterns of work (for example, more part time and 'flexible' contracts) may serve to reinforce the disadvantages faced by young people who experience difficulties in learning, or who have disabilities.

2.8 Fish stresses the value of inter-agency collaboration but he acknowledges that, even if services are well co-ordinated and working together towards clear aims, they might be rejected by young people themselves if their personal autonomy and control seem threatened. However, it remains a problem that many health and social services are provided, through the school system, for young people up to the age of sixteen and then stop. For transition to a meaningful life in the community, whether it be from school, college or a long-stay hospital, there has to be a support network to enable realistic choices to be made.

2.9 Fish shows how the 'Kurator' system in Denmark offers an exceptional level of continuity (Reader 2, p. 135). The 'Kurator' deals with the following:

(a) *School circumstances.* Choice of subjects, vocational orientation, work experience and placement, continued education, educational grants, youth schools.

(b) *Further education and training.* Continuation schools, evening schools, home economics schools, vocational schools, apprenticeships, basic vocational education and semi-skilled workers training schools.

(c) *Working conditions.* Choice of career, applications, references, salaries and conditions, careers officers, employers, trade unions and legislation.

(d) *Personal matters.* Disability, the home environment, economics, leisure time, accidents, military service, social security, public office and services and social welfare.

2.10 This approach is reflected in the *Code of Practice for the Identification and Assessment of Special Educational Needs* (DfE, 1994) to the extent that it too advocates a multidisciplinary approach which is recognized by many practitioners as being an effective way of working. However, it requires a commitment to develop the appropriate structures and resources to enable agencies to work collaboratively.

2.11 Fish illustrates the contradictory elements within services to support transition when he indicates that training for independence and employment may exist alongside a system which offers benefits for disabled people as long as they remain dependent or have 'unemployable' status. The temptation to accept dependency is powerful, especially if becoming more independent involves struggling with a whole range of bureaucratic systems in order to receive support towards that independence. The benefits system still promulgates a dependency model. Legislation such as the Disability Discrimination Act 1995 goes some way towards facilitating job opportunities by placing certain responsibilities on employers in relation to disability, but cuts in the Access to Work scheme, which supports employees, have been seen by some people as undermining the intentions of the Act and further disadvantaging disabled people within the job market (*TES*, 26 January 1996).

2.12 Fish suggests that the transfer of power from parents and professionals to individuals with disabilities can be problematic. This is a complex and contentious area. On the one hand parents and carers can be seen as having a key role in helping young people to generalize the social skills which they learn at college. On the other hand if professionals are to help young people make their own choices it can be argued that the level of parental involvement should be no greater than that of the parent or carer of any young student. The challenge for those working with students who experience difficulties in learning, or who have disabilities, is to help them to receive support from family or professionals without being suppressed by either. The aspirations of the individual concerned need to be kept at the centre of the process.

Activity 3 Rhetoric and reality in transition

Now read 'the rhetoric and reality of transition to adult life', by Jenny Corbett and Len Barton (Reader 2, Chapter 11).

As you read, consider the following questions:

- How are the concepts 'transition' and 'adult' defined? What criticisms do Corbett and Barton make of the way in which these concepts are generally used?
- How many rhetoric–reality gaps are there and what are they?

2.13   Corbett and Barton show that an understanding of 'transition to adulthood' must focus on an analysis of society and not just of the changes which need to take place within the individual young person who is making the transition.

2.14   They show that there is no fixed, single definition of 'adult status', as the concept is necessarily dependent on the social hierarchies within a culture. To focus on a narrow and undifferentiated view of adult status is to deny the influences of wealth, class, race and gender, as well as those of varying abilities, on the experience of transition. Affluent and well-educated parents may be able to offer more opportunities to their adolescent sons or daughters, so that their experience of transition is eased. Factors to do with class, gender and race still affect the extent of a young person's choice.

2.15   The authors also challenge the normalization philosophy which leads to statements such as that of the Council of Europe in 1986, which said that 'persons with mental handicaps ... should be able to lead as normal a life as possible'. By positing a fixed view of a 'normal' adult life such statements deny the particular identity of disabled people. Normalization policies are increasingly being challenged by the disability movement (see Jenny Morris, 1993 and Anne Chappel, 1990).

2.16   Throughout their chapter, Corbett and Barton show that there is a consistent gap between the rhetoric surrounding notions of transition to adulthood and the reality. They discuss four specific rhetoric–reality gaps:

- between a rhetoric of 'work' for young people and a reality of 'no choice' of employment;
- between a rhetoric of 'choice' of future career and a reality of economic and cultural 'devaluation';
- between a rhetoric of 'autonomy' and a reality of parental control and 'no opportunities';
- between a rhetoric of 'empowerment' and a reality of the 'invasion of privacy'.

2.17   Barton and Corbett show that definitions of adult status are culturally relative. It is often taken as an absolute truth that the development of individual autonomy is an essential feature of successful transition to adulthood, hence programmes for young people who experience difficulties in learning continually stress the importance of them gaining independence. However, in many cultures adult status is defined more by how far a person is able to play a full role within a social context and independent individualism is far less paramount (see Ingstad and Whyte, 1995). Even in a single society, notions of what defines adulthood vary considerably and are constantly changing. With high inner-city unemployment, do all young unemployed adults see themselves as not having achieved true adulthood, or have they found other indicators which mark their transition to a new role and status in life?

THE TRANSITION PROCESS IN EDUCATION: ADVICE CONTAINED IN THE CODE OF PRACTICE

2.18 Section 4 of Unit 1/2 is printed as a separate booklet, *How Should We React to Government Policies: responding to the Code of Practice*. The Code of Practice outlines the statutory responsibilities of LEAs and the governing bodies of maintained schools towards the children defined as having 'special educational needs'. It also offers guidance on carrying out these responsibilities, some of which is legally binding and some merely advisory. Guidelines for managing the transition process for pupils who have statements are given in the Code. The government's view of the importance of transition in educational terms for people who experience difficulties in learning, or who have disabilities may be judged from the fact that these guidelines are supported by Regulations carrying the force of law.

Activity 4 Transition in the Code of Practice

Now read the excerpt from the transition section of the Code of Practice in Appendix 1 (p. 62).

Note down the opportunities it offers of ensuring that the best interests of students are served. What might constrain its implementation?

2.19 The most significant opportunities that we identified were:

- to put the young person at the centre of the decision-making process;
- to emphasize as an essential prerequisite of autonomous transition the collaboration of the support agencies.

2.20 Most people pay lip service to the idea of choice but in reality there are many factors which preclude choice at 16, such as the contracting job market for this age group. In the absence of unemployment benefit they may have to accept government training schemes. Greater emphasis on accredited outcomes and a lack of vocational provision at foundation level or below has restricted the choice of further education courses now available to some young people. For most students classified as having serious learning difficulties, there may simply be no post-school educational provision available. For other groups there may be only one clear pathway, for example a specific college course, so while there is progression there is no choice.

2.21 In addition to limited options, actually making a choice may not be easy particularly for those who may not be able to think about the options. If they are to be meaningfully involved in decision making, more time will need to be given to the process and to consideration of how options can be presented, for example videos, visits and short 'taster' courses. In addition, there may be the need for comprehensive advocacy services for both young people and their parents.

2.22 The Code of Practice strongly promotes inter-agency collaboration. This is particularly necessary for young people who experience difficulties in learning, or who have disabilities, if they are to have their needs met in a holistic way. For example:

- Young people may need care supplied by Social Services in order for them to access educational provision.

- Young people with physical disabilities may feel they have to leave home if they are to achieve any personal autonomy. This will require the support and co-ordination of a variety of agencies.

- Young people with sensory impairments might need the support of specialist organizations, for example an RNIB College, but may wish to receive the bulk of their education within mainstream institutions.

2.23 Many practitioners recognize the importance of this collaboration but it is not always easy to put it into practice. First, the market economy in which practitioners function can mean that they have to work in an ethos of competition rather than collaboration. Secondly, the organizational structures and the focus of the agencies providing support often differ and may result in the emergence of conflicting priorities. Finally, unlike a statement, the transition plan is not a legally binding document. In this case, schools may have merely to demonstrate that they have paid 'due regard' to recommendations.

SUMMARY

2.24 Periods of transition in our lives may be accompanied by feelings of confusion and uncertainty about what the future might hold, but may cause even greater anxiety to the young people on the margins and/or their parents or carers. As Corbett notes, 'Transition is shaped by different opportunities and experiences and is a development which highlights inequalities' (Reader 2, p. 144). The increased attention paid to transition to adulthood in many countries is reflected in the emphasis given to the process of transition from school to further education training schemes or work in the Code of Practice. It is clear that many practitioners would wish to work within these recommendations but may not have the time and resources needed to implement them effectively. There is an irony in that, at a time of dwindling resources, practitioners are more frequently being set ideal standards but often lack the support needed to attain them.

3 FURTHER EDUCATION

3.1 In this section we begin with a brief historical overview of further education, outline the move to vocationalism, and go on to explore how the funding system determines the nature of provision. We then describe the range of provision in FE, the principle of support and support in practice, and, finally, discuss evaluation studies of this sector.

3.2 Students may have all sorts of reasons for enrolling on courses post-16, perhaps related to employment, individual interest or personal fulfilment. Education at this stage is not necessarily academic but may be increasingly related to vocational or work-based training or retraining. It is made up of a series of discrete programmes, each of which has its own outcome. The range of options open to young people is wide. For students who have a definite vocational or academic aim there are clear routes through existing vocational and A-level courses in both further education colleges and school sixth forms. However, what is available to students who experience difficulties in learning, or who have disabilities may be limited and not particularly well suited to their aptitudes or interests. Often the courses are less standardized and the breadth of the curriculum is dependent on the particular history and focus of an individual college.

3.3 Post-compulsory education takes place in a wide variety of locations – universities, further education colleges, community organizations, sixth forms in schools, sixth-form colleges, in the workplace and at home, through the media, open and distance learning and self-teaching. It can be full-time but is much more often part-time and is increasingly offered over an extended college year. Increasingly, school sixth forms are diversifying and allowing students to follow more vocational programmes. There is also a move in some areas for all sixth-form teaching to take place at a designated sixth-form centre. Many students choose to go directly to further education colleges, either because there is a wider range of courses on offer or because they wish to study in a more adult environment. The majority of students in further education are over 19.

THE DEVELOPMENT OF FURTHER EDUCATION

A historical perspective

3.4 Further education provision has often been developed piecemeal both in response to perceived needs and also in order to fit into funding requirements. In 1992 the Tomlinson Committee began to collect evidence for its subsequent report *Inclusive Learning* (FEFC, 1996). Up to this point, there had been no complete description of further education provision and very little research into the appropriateness of curricula. Interest in increasing access to further and higher education for all students does not have a long history. Moves towards equality of opportunity for all students in these sectors have tended to follow on from what was happening in schools.

3.5 Section 41 of the 1944 Education Act placed a duty on all local authorities to 'secure the provision for their area of adequate facilities for further education … for persons over compulsory school age'. Colleges of further education were originally designed as open institutions which could respond to local developments and provide:

> full-time and part-time education for persons over compulsory school age; and leisure time occupation in such organized cultural, training and recreative activities as are suited to their requirements for any persons over compulsory school age who are able and willing to profit by the facilities provided for that purpose.
>
> (Education Act 1944, Section 41)

3.6 As the demand for technical education grew in the mid-1950s, numbers of students in FE increased dramatically. When resources are scarce, some minority groups are ignored or neglected, and there was little provision made for students who experienced difficulty in learning. Students were expected to have the minimum standard of educational achievement to be able to follow the courses on offer. It was not until the mid to late 1970s in the context of increasing commitment to equal opportunities and human rights that the right of people who experience difficulties in learning to access further education began to be recognized and the first further education programmes for such people were established. The 1970 Education (Handicapped Children) Act required that a new group of students, those then categorized as 'severely sub-normal', should be included in schools and responsibility for them was transferred from local health authorities to education authorities. A similar act was passed Scotland four years later, and in Northern Ireland in 1987. This legislation led to a demand for further education for groups of students to whom previously it had been denied.

3.7 A survey undertaken in 1973 showed that only 10 per cent of those leaving special schools were taking courses in further education, while another 9 per cent were going to special residential colleges. However, during the 1970s, notions of educability for all students were accompanied by the development of basic education courses in further education colleges. In the 1980s the growth of the disability movement and the increasing politicization of disabled people themselves led to a growing demand for equal access to education for all disabled people within local colleges. Although some students who had previously been excluded did start to gain access to courses, this tended to be on an *ad hoc* basis. Access occurred on a modest scale and usually where students made minimal demands on physical resources and curricula provision. Most FE buildings were and still are physically inaccessible, as indicated in some FEFC inspection reports. The development of basic education courses was also encouraged by the Manpower Services Commission which was formed in 1974. Serious concern was expressed at the time about rising youth unemployment in particular because those who experienced difficulties in learning were increasingly disadvantaged by changes in the labour markets.

3.8 Initially colleges adopted a school-like approach to planning basic education courses and often recruited special school staff to deliver these programmes. During the seventies and eighties, several colleges created courses which were specifically designed to offer continuing education for groups of students with severe cognitive disabilities or who experienced some difficulties in learning. Sometimes these were closely socially integrated with the rest of the college – for example centrally placed in a major site – but at other times they were tucked away in an unobtrusive annexe. Several very exciting and innovative developments took place but provision was not spread evenly and its extent depended very much on the pressure particular groups of parents or school staff were able to exert on their LEA. Gradually there were also small but significant attempts to respond to the curriculum needs of these students at a national level and to identify good practice (Bradley, 1985).

3.9 The Education Reform Act of 1988 included a major section on 16 to 19 education. The Act saw curriculum entitlement in terms of obligations and rights in which providers were expected to enable learners to gain access to the resources they required (FEU, 1989). The National Union of Teachers reflected on the potential impact of the 1988 Act on the future provision for post-16 students:

> The 1988 Education Act appears to plug the loophole in the 1944 Education Act by making it the duty of every LEA to 'secure … adequate facilities in FE colleges' and to 'have regard to the requirements of persons over compulsory school age who have learning difficulties'. However, in conferring powers to LEAs to 'do anything which appears … necessary' for students with special educational needs, the 1988 Act allows local authorities to retain the element of choice as to the extent to which they use those powers.
>
> (NUT, 1990, pp. 2–3)

3.10 The Education Act of 1992 removed colleges of further education from the hands of the local authorities and established the Further Education Funding Council as the new funding body. The Act required the FEFC to 'have regard to the requirements of persons having learning difficulties' as it carries out its general duties of funding full and part-time provision. The expression 'shall have *regard to*' has been open to considerable comment and interpretation. How far do you feel that this terminology is likely to *guarantee* any student's rights to anything?

Activity 5   Changing perspectives in student support

Maureen Turnham made the transition from teacher to lecturer in 1984 and she has written about the changes that she, her students and the college have undergone since then.

Now read 'Supporting special needs in further education' by Maureen Turnham, which is Chapter 12 in Reader 2.

As you read, make some notes in answer to the following questions:

- What was Maureen Turnham originally employed by the college to do? How and why did her view of her job evolve and change?

- How did she set about reforming the curricula available to the students with learning difficulties and what obstacles did she face? How far was she able to overcome them?

3.11 Many staff in further education who were employed specifically to work with students with learning difficulties were, like Maureen Turnham, recruited from the special school sector. This had the advantage that they were experienced in providing support for learning but had the significant disadvantage that they knew nothing about the way in which further education operates. As Turnham recognizes, her naivety about the world of further education prevented her being able to adapt quickly. *She had to be integrated first before she integrated the students she was supporting.* As can be seen from her reflections, provision in colleges for disabled students has been *ad hoc* and often dismal, with the most makeshift and unsatisfactory conditions considered 'good enough' for this group.

3.12 The curriculum had developed over a period in which student numbers grew as careers officers were directing students towards the college. Where there is limited choice, this increase may be caused by students taking the only provision available rather than selecting the best or most appropriate. Turnham saw it as a healthy move when students began to cut the classes they found boring – in other words, to behave like 'normal' students. Her tale of the white ankle socks illustrates the problem of trying to define 'appropriate behaviour' for independent adults!

3.13 In order to have any lasting impact on the system, Turnham had to build bridges with management. Professional relationships were complex and intensely competitive, with inter-departmental rivalry requiring skilled political negotiation and calculating deals for resources. It is no wonder that staff who came in to support students who had a low status in the college were usually at the lowest lecturer grades and operating either solo or with very small teams of colleagues, in no position to become politically powerful; who is 'on your side' then becomes vitally important. As with the social workers in Islington in the mid-1980s whom you read about in Unit 5, if there is no top-down support for change, achieving an agreed or lasting policy may be impossible.

3.14 The demands of the 'market-place' within further education militate against providing adequate support for groups of students whose academic progress and economic prospects are unlikely to bring profit to the institution. Fighting for staffing, resources and opportunities for progression for these students can hardly be left to their support staff alone. What Turnham terms 'patchwork planning' is no longer adequate and her call is for 'a blueprint for services that have commitment, consultation and collaboration ingrained'. The now popular notion of 'entitlement' has to be seen as a civil right, backed by government legislation (as it is to some extent for children with statements in school).

3.15 Turnham insisted on calling her group 'life preparation' students. But this begs the question, 'What sort of life?'. While all other students in further education are following specific courses related to subject areas such as mathematics or French or to vocational areas such as carpentry, these students are preparing for life itself. This may be seen to emphasize their marginalized status in society and imply that they are not eligible for real life, as if being trained in the annexe prepares them for the 'annexe of life'.

3.16 However, what Turnham valuably records is that important changes were happening from 1984, when she started, until the time she was writing in 1991. Parent power was a force, making colleges offer a viable alternative to the training centres. Self-advocacy has led to a changed attitude towards students with learning difficulties. If they want to behave 'inappropriately', then why not? What is 'appropriate' behaviour for 16 to 19 year olds anyway?

3.17 Turnham shows that disabled students are oppressed, both by the kindness that awards them a childlike status and by the deep-rooted and simultaneous hostility that rejects them as full members of the college community.

3.18 Turnham reflects on her own acquiescence in a selection procedure that picked out for admission those students most likely to be acceptable in terms of their abilities and interests. She acknowledges that this was inequitable and contrary to her commitment to a policy of equal opportunities and to the countering of the fear, ignorance and prejudice that the students experienced in the college. She was aware that, if her colleagues came to accept her, then they were more likely to accept those they still saw as 'her' students.

The move to vocationalism

3.19 As we have already seen, the vast majority of students stay in education or employment-related training schemes after the age of 16. At the end of the 1980s the government expressed concern that UK standards of training had fallen significantly behind those of many other European countries. The National Council for Vocational Qualifications (NCVQ) was established to develop training standards in all vocational areas. 'Lead bodies' were set up by each industry to identify the particular skills needed by its own workforce. These skills have been listed as a series of 'competencies' to be achieved by trainees and accredited through national vocational qualifications (NVQs) from levels 1 to 5. At the beginning of their course students are given a list of statements which are intended to 'represent a common body of knowledge and understanding' among people working in that area. They are also given a list of 'performance criteria', the skills they must demonstrate when they are assessed. Ways in which they show they have these skills may be either practical or theoretical. They are called 'performance evidence'.

3.20   The system of assessment is complex as the following example shows. Katherine is working in a nursery and taking an NVQ level 2 in Child care and education – work in a pre-school group'. Her folder contains ten units of material, such as 'Care for children's physical needs', 'Support children's social and emotional development' and 'Carry out the administration of the provision for a care/education setting'. Each unit lists up to seven general skills ('performance criteria'), each one of which is subdivided into as many as nine statements of specific skills. If Katherine is to achieve the required accreditation for her work she must produce evidence of performance to meet each statement of specific skill within each general skill of each unit. She has attended college one day per week for one year of this course. She has not yet had any formal assessment of her work.

3.21   Since the advent of NVQs, general national vocational qualifications (GNVQs) have been introduced. GNVQs have an academic rather than a practical focus, within a particular vocational area, and are only offered at Levels 1–3. GNVQ Level 3 is often considered to be the vocational equivalent of the academic Advanced level GCSE.

3.22   A vocational approach to the education of teenagers may seem a sensible alternative to the traditional narrowly focused academic curriculum and a way of smoothing the transition from school to work. However, a serious general criticism of such schemes is that while they function to reduce the numbers of unemployed young people by occupying them in training, many trainees find no employment at the end of it and therefore see the training course as a waste of their time. Central government's motives behind promoting these schemes may also be questioned. The provision of government funding for training courses may serve to exonerate the government from blame for high levels of youth unemployment. When training courses are provided, blame shifts to the trainees if they do not join the course, or cannot subsequently find a job.

3.23   A number of criticisms have been made of the system of national vocational qualifications itself. A study by Sussex University researchers which surveyed 1,200 assessors and concentrated on NVQ Level 2 qualifications in construction, engineering and business administration was reported in *The Times Higher Education Supplement* of 29 November 1996. The leader of the research team, Michael Eraut, was quoted as criticising the cumbersome and bureaucratic nature of the assessment system, a funding framework that did not reflect the amount of training needed for trainees to achieve the required levels of competence, and individual work-based assessment that could not be used for the large numbers of candidates who received most of their training off the job. Of assessors, 38 per cent were reported to be passing 'substandard' students.

Other criticisms have also been made of a system of assessment which allows credit only for the pre-specified goals of the performance criteria and ignores both the processes of teaching and learning and any other student achievement on the course apart from those laid down. This system of vocational qualifications is directed by output, the kinds of competence laid down by the lead bodies. This is a major departure from previous approaches to education and training. Previously courses were governed by input of knowledge and skill development outlined in syllabuses. Now the outcomes of training programmes are specified as 'competencies', and outcomes generate income for those providing the training courses.

3.24 Despite such criticisms, government agencies identified national targets for education and training (NTETs) which incorporate these vocational qualifications. In 1995:

- by age 19, 63 per cent of young people achieved 5 GCSEs at Grade C or above, an intermediate GNVQ, or a full NVQ level 2;
- by age 21, 44 per cent of young people had achieved 2 A levels, an advanced GNVQ or a full NVQ level 3.

(DfEE, 1996c, p. 12)

3.25 NTETs have been set for the Year 2000 as

- by age 19, 85 per cent of young people to achieve 5 GCSEs at Grade C or above, an intermediate GNVQ, or a full NVQ level 2;
- by age 21, 60 per cent of young people to achieve 2 A levels, an advanced GNVQ or a full NVQ level 3.

(DfEE, 1996c, p. 13)

In addition, targets have been specified in communication, numeracy and information technology.

Table 1 Qualifications framework showing approximate equivalences between academic and vocational courses.

Academic	Vocational with academic focus	Vocational
Postgraduate and professional		NVQ Level 5
First degrees		NVQ Level 4
GCE A Level and AS Level	Advanced GNVQ	NVQ Level 3
GCSE	Intermediate GNVQ	NVQ Level 2
National curriculum pre-GCSE certificate of attainment	Foundation GNVQ	NVQ Level 1

3.26 Accrediting bodies have developed a plethora of pre-G/NVQ qualifications. These tend to emphasize a mixture of 'core' skills (for example social and communication skills) and specific vocational skills.

They also tend to follow the G/NVQ structure of competence-based assessment. A large number of colleges have chosen to accredit their programmes, particularly for students with greater cognitive disabilities, through the Open College Network. The Open College differs from other accrediting bodies in that it allows a particular institution to devise its own curriculum and then to have it validated within an agreed credit framework.

3.27   Staff seem to be attracted to this system for two reasons:

- they can maintain a broad-based curriculum;
- they can design an accredited curriculum which focuses on developing what the student can do rather than working towards the narrower criteria of competences defined by the National Council for Vocational Qualifications.

3.28   However, the disadvantage may be that it is more difficult to show student progression towards nationally recognized qualifications.

FUNDING FURTHER EDUCATION

3.29   The quality of the educational provision offered to students is inevitably bound to its funding. To a much greater extent than has traditionally been the case with education pre-16, provision post-16 is 'funding driven'. This means that resources in this sector are provided to support courses which meet pre-specified targets laid down by government agencies.

3.30   Since funding was centralized in England and Wales in 1992, most has come through government routes from a number of sources. This range of funding mechanisms reflects the complexity of post-compulsory education.

Centralized funding

The Further Education Funding Councils

3.31   There are two Further Education Funding Councils (FEFC), one for England and one for Wales. They are quangos which fund a substantial amount of further education and training as long as it fits into their criteria of externally accredited courses and qualifications. Scottish further education is funded through the Scottish Office Education Department. In 1992, further education colleges were taken out of LEA/borough control and were granted 'corporate status'. While they bid for funding from the FEFC, individual colleges manage these funds independently. The FEFC funds colleges per student per term on the basis of a thrice yearly census conducted in November, February and May, and mostly in proportion to qualifications pursued per student. Colleges also have a small funding element related to qualifications achieved and expressed in terms of funding units which are valued at between 4 per cent and 8 per cent of total recurrent funding.

European funding

3.32   Certain categories of European funding can be used to establish vocational training programmes particularly for groups who fall within recognized categories of disadvantage, for example long-term unemployed, people with disabilities and those living within an area of social deprivation.

Voluntary organizations

3.33   These organizations, for example the Royal National Institute for the Blind, often run day or residential training/education centres for people with specific disabilities. Such centres may receive funding from sources such as the FEFC or the Training Agency but this will be augmented by funding from the charitable parent organization.

Local funding

Local education authorities

3.34   LEAs still fund sixth forms. Local authority school sixth forms are funded through each LEA's own Local Management of Schools scheme. School sixth forms are funded mainly on the basis of pupil numbers through an annual census. Currently the funding of school sixth forms includes no differentiation by subject or by level or type of qualification. Grant-maintained school sixth forms are funded through the Funding Agency for Schools; currently there is no output-related funding element in the funding of school sixth forms, although performance tables have an influence on student recruitment. While students with statements remain in school, the LEA has to arrange the provision set out in the statement. A significant number of students with statements remain in maintained special schools until the age of 19, which are funded by the LEA through its Local Management of Special Schools scheme. Again, the LEA is responsible for arranging the provision on each student's statement.

3.35   Local authorities also fund a small amount of provision not specifically vocational or externally accredited, such as adult education classes.

Implications of variation in funding

3.36   Individual learner needs are funded differently in the various sectors. Under local authority schemes, schools are generally allocated additional funds for students 'with special educational needs' if they have a statement. Some local authorities use proxy indicators, such as the numbers of free school meals, to allocate resources to schools for non-statemented students who experience difficulties. In the FE sector, the extra support required for students 'with learning difficulties and/or disabilities', its cost and confirmation of its delivery must be written in a document which can be audited to support colleges' claims for additional resources.

3.37 Up to 1996, one of the major differences between sixth forms and other providers has been that funding in schools is not tied to the level of the course being followed by the student, or by the output achieved or to regular attendance. However, in June 1996 the Government committed itself to change this situation to:

> secure greater convergence of funding arrangements for school sixth forms, FE sector colleges and work-based training, including the introduction of an element of output-related funding for school sixth forms
>
> (DfEE, 1996a)

3.38 Subsequently it published a consultation document, *Funding 16–19 Education and Training: Towards Convergence,* whose aim was 'to identify the principles of funding systems which promote the standard of students' learning, opportunities, competition between providers, value for money in public expenditure on education, choice in different kinds of provision' (DfEE, 1996b). Whether 'convergence' will serve the interests of all students well in bringing about greater equality of opportunity, or will have the effect of making some students less popular to providers remains to be seen.

3.39 In addition to the many different sources of funding the modes of funding also vary. Some, such as European funds, have to be bid for in a competitive market, some are related only to specific projects and much non-FEFC is short-term. A great deal of managers' time is taken up with manipulating these sources of funding and the range of provision on offer may have less to do with statutory rights and more to do with how creatively a particular organization can successfully exploit the potential resources available. This is especially true when providing for students whose requirements do not fit the mainstream qualification framework.

Limitations of the FEFC system of funding

Pressure to achieve recognized qualifications

3.40 The FEFC established its curriculum criteria very much within the context of the existence of NTETS and the pressure to increase the number of people who achieve nationally recognized qualifications. This had a big impact on provision for students who experience difficulties in learning. Despite strong lobbying, the National Council for Vocational Qualifications set its lowest strand of accreditation at a level which was still beyond the reach of many students who experience difficulties in learning. The degree of core skills required, the ability to complete multiple choice tests and the high level of consistency required by the competencies made even the first rung of the vocational qualification ladder too high for some students to step on to.

3.41   Schedule 2 of the Further and Higher Education Act 1992 listed courses eligible for funding by the Further Education Funding Council. It also described the criteria for eligibility for funding for each one. The courses listed included academic and vocationally accredited programmes. When the Act was being considered it omitted consideration of students who could not qualify for academic or vocational courses. Following lobbying by pressure groups such as Skill (the National Bureau for Students with Disabilities) a paragraph was added which allowed for courses in:

> independent living and communication for those with learning difficulties which prepare them for entry to (other specified) courses.
>
> (Further and Higher Education Act 1992, Schedule 2, paragraph j)

3.42   Courses in 'independent living and communication for those with learning difficulties' are described as eligible for funding only if they *'prepare'* students *'for entry to'* other courses which offer:

- vocational qualification;
- GCSE or GCE A/A level;
- 'access' for entry to a course of higher education;
- basic literacy in English
- English where English is not the language spoken at home;
- basic principles of mathematics.

3.43   The inclusion of paragraph 2j was an extremely important and welcome addition to the curriculum criteria. However, when one scrutinizes the paragraph, it becomes apparent that what allows a particular learning programme to be funded is the perceived ability of students on it to eventually achieve a nationally recognized qualification which will enable them to progress to another FEFC-funded programme. Positive progression, which is a specified criterion for funding, is only seen in educational terms, i.e., the ability to move on to one of the qualifications listed in Schedule 2(d) to (g). While 'independent living' is cited as a possible *component* of the programme, living independently is not recognized as a positive outcome, nor are employment or enhanced quality of life. In effect, provision for students with the highest level of need, for example those who experience very serious difficulties in learning as a result of profound and complex cognitive disabilities, does not meet these criteria. While courses for students with severe or moderate learning difficulties might be able to be integrated into the system and included in the framework, the framework itself has become more exclusive.

3.44   The Dearing Committee (1996) acknowledged that there is a general need to recognize the apparently small achievements which for many young people represent substantial advances.

> To cater for the full range of pupils, it may be necessary to develop units of work written specifically for individuals or groups which are then accredited and recognized formally.
>
> (Dearing, 1996, para. 12.47)

> Courses to accredit skills for independent adult life should be developed against ... nationally recognized criteria, drawn up by the regulatory bodies with approval from the Secretaries of State ... These should be at the entry level in the proposed National Framework ... In addition the regulatory bodies should devise simple quality assurance measures for schemes to accredit small, worthwhile steps of progress by those with severe learning difficulties.
>
> (Dearing, 1996, para. 12.51)

Purchase of expensive equipment

3.45   Funding cannot be claimed from the FEFC for buying equipment or adapting buildings. If colleges need to provide access, for example for a wheelchair user who needs to reach the laboratories on the third floor where there is no lift, or to acquire equipment, for example for a visually impaired student who requires a close circuit television and computer adaptations to be able to read and write, they can refuse such students entry unless they can fund these changes from non-FEFC resources. When we were writing this, it was too early say whether test cases arising out of the 1995 Disability Discrimination Act would alter this situation.

Emphasis on student attendance and retention

3.46   Colleges may be even less willing to risk accepting the significant number of students who have already had problems fitting into the educational system, and there is no compulsion on them to do this. Keele University figures indicate that 20 per cent of students in their last year of compulsory schooling truanted regularly, and 25 per cent of secondary pupils sometimes or often 'behave badly' (Barber, 1994). Colleges are more likely to exclude students whose behaviour is seen as challenging because of the increasing emphasis on student attendance, retention and completion levels.

3.47   The Dearing Committee took the view that groups of students experiencing difficulties of this kind must have their needs taken seriously (in a paragraph in which one could replace 'under-achievers' with 'working class' or 'black' students):

> Under-achievers may be of any ability. They characteristically have the potential to achieve considerably more, but fall behind for a variety of reasons, such as disaffection, truancy, severe difficulties at home, or personal psychological problems ... The prospects for such young people in the next century are poor. Educational attainment will be increasingly a pre-condition of employment. Under-achievers

> who cannot find or keep jobs may become disaffected citizens. In turn, there is a risk that they will pass their attitudes to their children. The children of parents with low standards of literacy tend to find themselves at a disadvantage at school ... Such pupils become more likely to be excluded from school and may end up in an educational limbo, relying on a few hours a week of home tuition or part-time attendance at a Pupil Referral Unit.
>
> (Dearing, 1996, paras 12.24–6)

3.48 Dearing recommends that vocationally orientated courses should be introduced at 14+ to re-awaken the interest of disaffected pupils. 'Their greatest need is to succeed and regain some self-esteem, after what may have been years of being seen as a failure at school' (Dearing, 1996, 12.36). Current funding arrangements for the FE sector do not resource the attendance of 14 year olds at colleges. The school environment is therefore nominated in the report as the centre for the student's 'continued development'. Theoretically it allows the student to access the broad, balanced curriculum followed by everyone else. However, it implies that students will continue to attend the school where they have already failed for so long. Should some other alternative be considered? Should we perhaps consider how to encourage a more inclusive climate in mainstream schools for all students at a much earlier stage?

SUPPORT AND PARTICIPATION

3.49 With the establishment of the FEFC, the interpretation of what was 'adequate' provision for students who need support is now the choice not of the LEAs but of the newly incorporated individual colleges. Colleges were no longer funded for courses but for individual students who attracted funding units.

3.50 The FEFC established an 'Additional Support Fund' specifically to address the diverse range of identified individual student need. The need for extra resources was defined as arising from a perceived difficulty in learning, a disability, or a need for additional assistance in acquiring English as a second language or in basic literacy and numeracy skills. This was the first time that funding for support was designated at this level and was useful for students with disabilities who wished to access mainstream programmes. However, it had significant limitations in that capital costs for equipment and structural adaptation of buildings were not included within it.

3.51 Many colleges have extensive additional provision to support students. Support is often managed by separate basic skills, English as a second language and access co-ordinators and may take the form of both separate provision and on-course support. Because further education can constitute a second chance for many of its students who may have been failed by the school system, a very high proportion of its students can be said to have experienced some difficulty with learning, so the majority of provision is built around identified support strategies.

The range of provision

3.52   Although the FEFC laid down specific criteria for funding, there is still wide variation of provision for students.

Learning support within local FE colleges

3.53   A survey by the Basic Skills Agency showed that around 15 per cent of a representative sample of 21 year olds have significant difficulties with basic literacy and numeracy (Bynner and Steedman, 1995). The FEFC's method of funding enables individual students to receive additional learning support as part of their individual learning programme. Such support can take a huge variety of forms. For example, deaf students may require significant input from a communicator, while other students may only require a small amount of help – for example, an hour a week from a tutor who may assist students with written assignments. The type and level of support is decided through negotiation between student, course tutor and support tutor. Students are working within an adult context and, although support may be strongly recommended by staff, individual students do not always choose to take it up.

Designated provision within local FE colleges

3.54   Many day colleges have also created courses specifically designed for students who experience difficulties in learning. These can take a variety of forms. Some have grown out of the models developed in the seventies and eighties and emphasize the importance of a broad curriculum framework which encourages students to develop their social and independence skills through taking part in a wide range of curricula activities, for example communications, basic skills, cookery and life skills, sports, creative studies and independent travel. Others concentrate on preparing students for progression to vocational training. The course context tends to be determined by what a particular college offers and the demands made by local special schools, rather than being developed according to an overall, external strategy.

3.55   Sometimes such courses are separate from those for students who are not categorized as having learning difficulties – students may be based in a segregated part of the building. In others, students share the same area but are taught in separate groups. Some colleges have students being taught partially within discrete tutorial groups and then joining a wider range of students for other parts of the curriculum. The amount of integration open to students often depends on what the college offers overall – for example how wide a range it has of vocational options accredited at a relevant level.

3.56   Courses run for adults in basic literacy and numeracy skills, often termed 'adult basic education' (ABE), can be run by local training providers, for example an FE college, and funded through the FEFC if they can be shown to be directed towards an accredited outcome, for example a certificate of competence at some level, and/or if they allow students to progress on to other courses. To many students, however, gaining a certificate may seem irrelevant to what they want from taking the course. A tutor responsible for an adult literacy course in an East Midlands county spoke about her perception of why adults may suddenly decide that they want to be able to read better:

> It's often because they have reached a crisis point, a sudden period of unemployment, for example. They can't get away without literacy all of a sudden. Crises to do with unemployment mostly affect men. They are suddenly faced with paperwork – forms, cards – and it starts hitting home. They are referred to us by the unemployment service. We advertise in the Job Centres. There is a lot of embarassment with illiteracy. It involves both men and women. Men find it harder to reveal. They often cry. Their feelings about not being able to read are also to do with their not being able to look after their families properly. Women don't cry. It is more stigmatizing for a man, especially if they have to reveal it to their own children. They have feelings of inadequacy. Their perception of what society thinks of them is that they are thick. They're faced in banks and post offices and other public places with failure. There is a lot of anger and resentment at themselves and at others – often the person behind the counter. This can bring them into adult education …

> Some adults want to help their own children. One parent said to me: 'When my 7 year old son told me how to sound a word out I decided this was the time. But coming through the door for the first time was awful …'

Residential colleges

3.57   Every year a significant minority of students will leave school and move on to specialist residential colleges. Individual student places may be funded by the FEFC but the colleges themselves have often been established by voluntary organizations, for example Manor House FE College, Torquay, and New College Worcester run by the Royal National Institute for the Blind (RNIB). Fees are banded according to the student's support needs. The FEFC will only fund placements if it has been established that appropriate education cannot be provided by the local FE college. For students to receive FEFC funding at residential colleges they have to follow an accredited programme. This is augmented by the social and leisure activities which make up the rest of the provision.

3.58   Recently such institutions have been heavily criticised by some sections of the disability movement, often on the assumption that they work according to a medical model of disability and isolate students from the mainstream. However, students themselves are often very positive about aspects of their residential placement, emphasizing the very high level of specialist support they receive, the importance of being able to establish an identity with a peer group who have a similar experience of disability, and for some, the importance of being able to move away from home (Skill, 1996). The quality of their experiences clearly depends on the individual institution. The colleges themselves are recognizing the

Communicating needs: Students in a residential special college

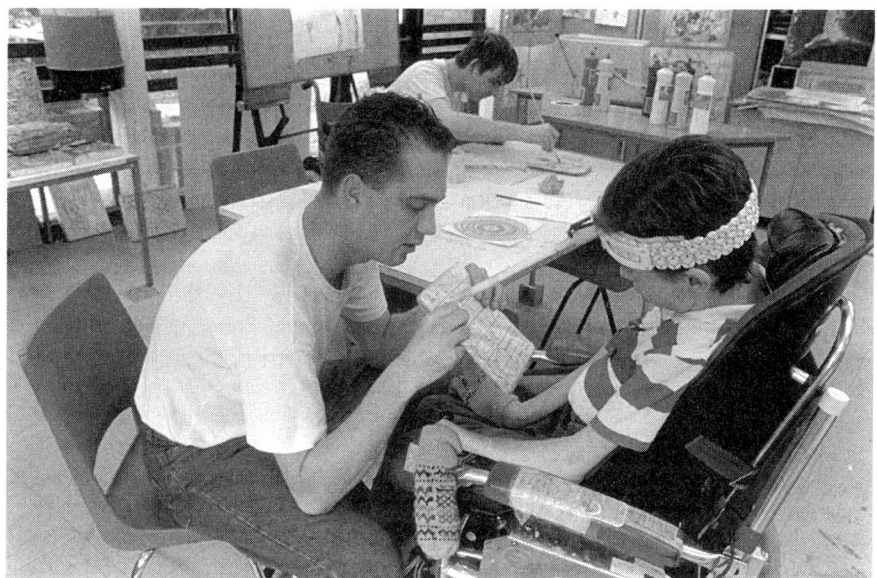

Communicating with the tutor in an art class.

Communicating with care staff in the lunch break.

importance of offering opportunities for students to work with a wider peer group and there are many examples of them working with local FE colleges to extend the range of provision and student choice.

3.59 The three approaches above are not mutually exclusive. As we have seen, residential colleges are increasingly joining with local colleges to widen their curriculum. Some students from separate course are moving on to mainstream provision with additional support and others are for the first time experiencing non-segregated educational provision.

Activity 6 Comparing integrated and designated provision

Read the description of provision in two colleges in Appendix 2. Consider the following questions:

1. Could each approach be successful in including all students within the mainstream of education?
2. What important aspects of a student's learning experience might be excluded by either approach?

Strengths of each approach

3.60 'Inclusion' in this course is defined as a process of increasing the participation of all students in the mainstream of education and reducing their exclusion from it. The strengths of the fully integrated approach have been listed by the learning support manager of Blackburn College. They include:

- students having access to a wider choice of vocational options;
- students joining courses that have equal status – i.e. are not seen as 'special needs' provision;
- working towards a change of attitude in other staff and students;
- moving away from the notion of negative labelling;

3.61 In the Lewisham project special provision was made for the 'designated' group of students. It can therefore only be said to increase the participation in the mainstream of these students if the project itself is considered an integral part of the college, if the students have the choice as to whether to join the project or take some other course, and if completion allows progress on to other mainstream courses. Given those provisos, the Lewisham project's strengths might be said to include:

- offering provision that is specifically geared to the needs of the student group;
- learning on an equal basis, i.e. individual students not requiring significantly more support than other students on the course;
- strong peer group support from students with similar interests and abilities;

- being part of a successful programme which raises the status of both students and staff through their involvement in high profile cross-college activities.

Aspects of a student's learning experience that could be excluded

3.62   The learning support manager at Blackburn indicated two potential disadvantages to their provision. Blackburn College is highly vocational with a wide range of practical skills offered at NVQ Level One. All students were enabled to participate in this diverse curriculum at a level to suit themselves. The concept of inclusion cannot be divorced from what the college offers overall. Colleges that have a more academic/business orientation might find an integrated approach hard to replicate because they may be unused to differentiating teaching materials and approaches to meet students' needs. Another question which must be asked about the fully integrated approach is the extent to which it can accommodate the full range of students' learning needs. It is unclear whether students with great cognitive impairment would be able to take an active role. Pozyganza might not be able to accommodate those students either, but a college which is positive about specialized provision might be more able to meet the very high demands of that student group within a specifically designed course. A college that adheres to total integration could end up excluding some students unless they had access to extra support and equipment. A final aspect of the students' learning experience is peer-group support and equal interaction. A student receiving high levels of support within his/her main programme of study could be made to feel different and not experience student-to-student interaction in the same way as someone learning independently.

3.63   We have already said that the Lewisham project may tend to segregate students in that it has special students being taught by specialist staff in a specialist base room. It could be argued that these students are being denied equality of opportunity and access to a wider range of vocational specialisms. The project is certainly on quite a small scale. There is also a possibility that this model could reinforce a situation where students only achieve success because they are part of a special group and are not competing on the same terms as everybody else.

3.64   Dee and Maudslay felt that there was a place for both approaches depending on what the college offered overall and the needs, abilities and wishes of individual students. What is important is how far students could participate in activities integral to the mainstream provision. Added to this is the quality of the educational programmes provided and the benefits and choice which they bring to the students by enabling them to achieve positive outcomes and progression and by enhancing the overall quality of their lives.

Link courses

3.65   One of the ways intended to encourage a smooth transition from statutory to post-compulsory education is the provision of link courses in which students spend some of their final school year in college on specially designed programmes. Through such courses college staff can assess student need and the suitability of the proposed full-time course in a real situation. The best link courses form part of a transition curriculum jointly designed by school and college staff and the students. For students who feel disenchanted with the school system, the chance to be in a more adult situation can make them want to give a second chance to formal education. Staff have the opportunity to co-ordinate an effective programme of support for students before they attend full time. Such support can include both specialist staffing, for example an interpreter for a deaf student, or extra equipment, for example technical aids for someone who is visually impaired.

3.66 Link courses can run in a variety of ways. They can be blocks of several days or weeks or they can take place one or two days a week over a number of terms. Some link courses are attached to a specific full-time programme – for example a disabled student attending college one day a week may spend some of the time with fellow school leavers and the rest with students who are already attending the full-time course. Students may have an opportunity to negotiate a contract covering the structure and content of their learning programme. This may give them a level of choice and control which they may not have had in school.

3.67 The funding of link courses is problematic. When both schools and further education were under the auspices of the LEA it ultimately paid for the provision. Currently, with schools being funded by the LEAs and colleges largely by the FEFC, there is room for dispute. The FEFC has made it clear that it is legally unable to be responsible for students under the age of sixteen if they are in receipt of full-time schooling, but schools are often unwilling or unable to pay what might be a substantial sum out of their budget. This has meant that several innovative and successful link programmes have had to close. However, in some cases staff and parents have lobbied very strongly for the schools and LEAs to pick up the bill. The effectiveness of this lobbying shows that it is possible for funds to be found.

EVALUATING FURTHER EDUCATION

Students' views

3.68 But what do the students themselves say about the quality of provision on offer? Why did they enter FE? Were their reasons different from other students?

3.69 As part of the process of information collection by the Tomlinson Committee, the FEFC commissioned Skill, the National Bureau for Students with Disabilities, to run a series of workshops for students 'with learning difficulties/disabilities' to provide the Committee with first hand evidence of the views and experiences of students in FE (Skill, 1996). In these workshops students reported that on the whole the motivation to enter further education had come from themselves, rather than parents. They saw further education as providing qualifications, and helpful for employment or access to higher education. However, reasons concerned with their own personal development were often of greater significance to them. They mentioned the opportunities provided by further education to pursue their own interests and its contribution to the development of independence, social life and self-confidence.

3.70   Overall the students felt their experiences would benefit them, but there was a feeling that general further education provision in particular was not yet geared to the needs of people 'with learning difficulties and disabilities'. Managers did not appear to understand the problems associated with particular forms of disability. Equipment and materials were not always either available, in a fit condition to be used, or appropriate for the students' use, particularly for those with dyslexia and visual impairments. Students with learning difficulties were particularly concerned about unreliable, inflexible and expensive transport arrangements. A number of students reported difficulty with physical access to college facilities such as canteens and libraries because of the lack of lifts or because doors were too heavy for them to move. Sometimes general FE education schedules did not make sufficient provision for the extra time required by disabled students to eat and to use the toilet.

3.71   The transition from school to general FE had been stressful for some students for a number of reasons. They had not been ready for the amount and quality of work expected from FE courses, and they were not used to being given freedom and being treated more like adults. Those from residential schools also found it hard to cope in a situation where they were in the minority amongst non-disabled students. The easiest transitions had occurred when students already had friends in FE, the class contained students who experienced similar difficulties in learning and/or disabilities, and tutors understood and were prepared for the requirements of students.

3.72   Funding arrangements for providing additional support for students in further education are tied to identification and assessment of specific needs and then costing the extra support requirements needed for students to reach their individual targets. Participants in the workshops expressed views about issues concerning the assessment process itself as well as the use of labels which a process of this kind may encourage. Many said they had been confused by the assessment that had been carried out, especially at FE institutions without discrete teaching units. There was often a delay before support was provided because the assessment itself had not taken place quickly enough after enrolment; sometimes the assessment itself was not comprehensive enough to assess needs fully. Sometimes, also, no notice was taken of what the student wanted. However, some students who describe themselves as dyslexic or visually impaired commented that enrolment in FE was the first opportunity that had ever been given to discuss fully the difficulties they experienced in accessing the curriculum and the support arrangements they would like.

3.73 Students expressed a diversity of views on the use of labels to refer to 'difficulties in learning and/or disabilities'. Everybody objected to the terms 'mental handicap' and 'handicapped' which were felt to be devaluing and did not indicate what kind or amount of additional support a student needed. Generally they acknowledged that labels can be useful for identifying situations where extra provision is needed to overcome difficulties, for example where a blind student needs Braille equipment. Avoidance of labels could sometimes be counter-productive. They considered specific labels which indicated a single specific disability, for example blindness and dyslexia, were acceptable because they described the problem itself and gave an indication of what was necessary to help the student concerned. Other people's ignorance and fear of what in the context of further education is termed 'learning difficulties and/or disabilities' were seen to discriminate against disabled students.

3.74 Participants in the workshops felt that residential colleges provide high quality, individually-tailored support, but inadequate opportunities to mix with non-disabled people.

3.75 General further education colleges have the benefits of an integrated environment but feelings of social isolation for some disabled students in an non-disabled environment and frequent incidence of inadequately-met support needs.

3.76 Students felt that overall what they wanted was 'tailor-made help and an integrated environment' (Skill, 1996, p. 3).

Activity 7 Setting the agenda for empowerment

Some colleges have deliberately set out to empower students in decision-making about provision made for them. In 'Setting the agenda: student participation on a multi-media learning scheme' (Reader 1, Chapter 6), Stuart Olesker describes a course that began in 1982 and is, essentially, a specialized course for a separated population of students. However, these students devise their own projects. They are encouraged to develop collaboration across courses with students working at a range of academic levels and they participate in a self-assessment strategy by preparing their own 'portrait portfolios'.

Read the chapter, making some notes in answer to the following questions:

- What does 'empowerment' mean in the context of the students on the Portsmouth multimedia learning scheme?
- In what ways do the form and the content of the multimedia scheme very from what you know of FE college courses? What are its most important features?
- In what ways are students integrated into college life?
- In what ways other than strictly educational do the students on the scheme stand to benefit?

- Are there disadvantages for students on the scheme?
- How has Stuart Olesker, a lecturer, attempted to bring alive the experience of his students in the way he has written his chapter?

3.77   Empowerment is not just about exercising choice, as it has sometimes been portrayed, but is also about active participation, such as during the multimedia scheme meeting. It is demanding and difficult. It will not accommodate pre-planned teaching objectives and curriculum frameworks. As the chapter shows, a wide range of educational, political and social issues are raised by students as urgent concerns, including 'next term's curriculum'. The students can work with staff to define and prioritize their own needs. The approach is radical in the sense that students have come into the scheme knowing what they do not want, having already rejected the conventional pattern proposed for them.

3.78   Stuart Olesker and his colleagues encourage 'error-permitted learning'. So many courses for these students have clearly set teaching objectives which they either achieve or fail. If it is anticipated that they will fail, they might not be allowed to take the risk. Individualized programmes may be negotiated by staff and students, but students are guided within an initial assessment of their skills. 'Error-permitted learning' implies that it is the learning process itself which is of value and that making errors is a valuable part of that process.

3.79   Through joint work with students working towards a range of qualifications, the multimedia students are encouraged to value their own ideas and to engage collaboratively in practical designs which will meet their immediate and long-term needs. As an exercise in empowerment it could not be more relevant. They are valued in high quality and imaginative tasks which they would not be able to do alone. The projects are useful and, through this process, the personal becomes political.

3.80   Students like Jane take responsibility for others who may have more severe disabilities and, through a shared experience, help to make all their lives more interesting and sociable. The use of the 'portrait portfolios' enables many diverse aspects of the students' lives to be part of their learning experience. The notion of success or failure in achieving specific tasks is irrelevant and that narrow definition of learning meaningless. The promotion of 'appropriate behaviours', which is an integral part of many special college courses training students to develop social skills, is here challenged. We see the student group behaving with maturity and tolerance over what, in another context, might be seen as an unacceptable tantrum from one of their fellow students.

3.81   As Stuart Olesker says, this scheme, which is open, accessible and encourages 'celebration of differences', is dangerous in that 'this will attract problems of security, focus and organization' (p. 82). Yet the element of risk inherent in allowing student empowerment is surely compensated for by the unexpected emergence of talents which such an approach permits. It is the unpredictability of the scheme which allows it to be an 'educational' experience for the students, rather than a 'training' experience.

3.82   Apart from the educational benefits of the scheme, Stuart Olesker notes that students are supported to overcome depression and to make constructive use of their anger. They are enabled to raise their expectations of their own capabilities. He presents his discussion as if through the eyes of a potential student, 'Michael' – not quite a first-person account and not quite a third-person account. Did you find the style effective? Would it have been better if the students' own voices could have been heard more loudly?

3.83   Olesker's experiences are not yet typical and many FE colleges retain a skills-based, more tightly structured programme for their special courses, which are rarely integrated in the manner he describes. Patterns of course provision vary according to college policy and historical accident.

The Tomlinson review

3.84   In 1992, following the Further and Higher Education Act, a committee under Professor John Tomlinson was established to investigate further education provision for particular groups of students. The brief of this Committee was to:

- examine current provision for the 130,000 students 'with learning difficulties and/or disabilities' in FE;
- say whether the legal requirements of the Act were being fulfilled;
- make recommendations for remedies if they were not being satisfied.

3.85   However, Professor Tomlinson says in his introduction that there was also a 'deeper purpose ... to extend further education to thousands not now included'

3.86   The Committee commissioned a review of the research literature and a 'nationwide mapping' of provision, and took evidence from many involved in further education. It concluded that students who experience difficulties in learning have a poorer deal than others in terms of the quality of provision.

> ... there is clear evidence that many groups are under-represented, including adults with mental health difficulties, young people with emotional and behavioural difficulties and people of all ages with profound and multiple disabilities. For those who *are* taking part, the quality of provision is not good enough.
>
> ...
>
> But there is also clear evidence that the quality of the provision made for these students is less good than that to be found in colleges generally. The work seldom features in college-wide systems of strategic planning, quality assurance or data collection and analysis. Few questions are asked about the purpose or relevance of what students with learning difficulties and/or

disabilities are being asked to learn. Monitoring and evaluation of students' achievements is less common in this work than elsewhere and managers often lack awareness or understanding of what is required.

(FEFC, 1996, pp. 10 and 6)

3.87 The report points out that:

Involvement in productive economic activity of people of working age with disability is one-half that of those without disability (40 per cent compared with 83 per cent). Two-fifths (41 per cent) of disabled people of working age have no educational qualifications compared with under one-fifth (18 per cent) of non-disabled people … unemployment rates … among people with disabilities are around two and a half times those for non-disabled people (21.6 per cent compared with 9 per cent).

(FEFC, 1996, p. 7)

3.88 The difficulties that people have faced as a result of their disabilities have been reinforced by 'low educational opportunities'. One of the reasons given for the poorer quality of what is on offer to these students is that the level of training of their teachers is not good enough and must be improved.

3.89 Tomlinson recommended an inclusive approach to further education which the report defined as 'redesigning the very processes of learning, assessment and organization so as to fit the objectives and learning styles of the students' (p. 4) rather than designing the courses first and then giving some students extra help to enable access. You will notice that this definition is different from that in E242 – the definition of inclusion used in the report is the greatest degree of match or fit between individual learning requirements and provision.

3.90 The report identifies the first step in reconceptualizing provision as the acknowledgement that all students have the same learning needs:

The first step is to determine the best possible learning environment, given the individual student and learning task … We envisage a system that is inclusive and that will require many mansions. Each element of the system will need to play its part …

(FEFC, 1996, p. 5)

3.91 The Committee adopted the principle that 'everyone who can benefit from further education should be able to participate'; that 'further education provision should match the individual requirements of those who might participate'; and that 'the further education sector should work in conjunction with other providers to ensure a pattern of provision which maximizes participation' (FEFC, 1996, pp. 53–4).

3.92 The Committee took very seriously the views of the students who were asking for a greater degree of self advocacy. There was overt acknowledgement in the report that students have had insufficient control over their own future educational experiences. The report recommended that the students themselves should specify how they find learning difficult. The 'assessment of students' requirements' should be

- guided by the students' wishes: the assessment process should offer opportunities ... to the individual ... to make their views and wishes known and to influence decision-making;
- fair; the assessment process should be impartial and take into account individual differences including any effect of the student's ethnicity, gender and age in relation to their disability or learning difficulty;
- transparent; the purpose, criteria and outcomes ... should be understood by the student ... or advocates.

(FEFC, 1996, p.74)

3.93 In addressing the issue of collaboration between colleges and agencies concerned with individual students, the committee again supported greater self-advocacy by students. The report said that effective collaboration is based on the principle that 'individuals have the right to say what they want to do with their lives' and that 'individuals' aspirations should be respected and acted upon by the organizations that work with them' (FEFC, 1996, p. 120).

3.94 Tomlinson also addressed the issue of organizing the funding of FE to bring about greater equality of opportunity for all students.

> Our most radical proposal is that the Council should urge the Government to establish a common funding base for all post-16 education whether in schools or in further education. We have been convinced that current differences affecting students with learning difficulties make no sense in educational terms and are not in the public interest because they only add to the anxieties of students and their families or advocates at times when choice should be based solely on the quality and appropriateness of educational provision.

(FEFC, 1996, p. 10)

Notions of inclusion

3.95 The definition of inclusion in Unit 1/2 of this course is that it is a *process* of increasing the participation and reducing the exclusion of all students in the mainstream of education. Placing all students within the generally available provision may give the illusion that everyone has the opportunity to participate in the education offered by a college. However, we need to question how far current provision can meet the needs of all students.

Activity 8 Exploring notions of inclusion in FE

Read Appendix 3, which is an extract from an article by Maudslay and Dee. Note that the authors use the phrase 'including all students' to mean something different from the definition of inclusion in E242, where it is seen as a process.

Note down your responses to the following questions:

- What are the practicalities of making appropriate provision for all students in further education?
- What is the 'skewed polarity' and why do the authors think it is not a helpful way of looking at the issues?
- What aspects of the curriculum may be excluded if students are only given access what is currently available?
- What examples are there in further education of courses that are run for discrete groups?
- What is the difference between 'normalization' and 'quality of life'?

3.96 Maudslay and Dee suggest that the practicalities of including all students are closely linked to the organization and structure of further education and that effective inclusion would be dependent upon fundamental changes to the mainstream college curriculum. They acknowledge the extensive changes which have occurred in further education over the past few years. The most significant of these is the establishment of the FEFC. The authors suggest that this, combined with a greater emphasis on the achievement of national training targets, the drive towards external accreditation and the linking of outcomes to funding may lead institutions to compete for students who will cost less to teach and earn the institution more. They also suggest that developments such as individual learning programmes, modularization and the differentiation of teaching styles and support structures, all of which would increase the accessibility of the curriculum to students who experience difficulties in learning, are still relatively rare within the mainstream of colleges.

3.97 The authors say instead that the vision of inclusion itself demands clear definition. You may feel that the definition of inclusion in E242 meets that requirement. Maudslay and Dee feel that what is required is not a stark contrast between integration being seen as 'good' and segregation being seen as 'bad'. They refer to this 'skewed polarity' as one which makes many assumptions about the content and organization or provision but which does not effectively examine the framework of further education and the extent to which it enables students to follow patterns of learning which are appropriate to their individual requirements.

3.98 Elsewhere, Maudslay and Dee quote McGinty and Fish saying 'that … education must be aimed at informed adulthood, life-long learning and concern for others as well as vocational proficiency.' However, increasing vocationalism could lead to important aspects of the curriculum being lost as core skills and cross-curricula themes, which very often give students the skills they need to move into work-related training, give way to earlier and earlier specialization.

3.99 The narrowing of the curriculum already often fails to meet the needs of those with more severe and complex impairments. In addition, people who have experienced learning and behavioural difficulties in schools may reject a qualification-based pathway in favour of low-paid work or unemployment. Whether it is the system that rejects them or they who reject the system, the extent to which potential students are already excluded needs to be addressed.

3.100 Maudslay and Dee argue that there is a need for high quality educational provision that enables all students to participate, progress and achieve. They cite 'access courses' as an example of such provision in that they 'allow learners ... to regain their place in an educational system'. Maudslay and Dee give other examples of where, for some of the time, people may benefit from being able to identify themselves as a distinct group and from being offered the opportunity to study with their own chosen peer group. The Danish example is interesting because it stems not from the assumption that 'normality' and 'commonality' are automatically desirable but from the belief that 'quality of life' and the potential for people to 'follow their own convictions and shape their own lives' may be better goals.

3.101 Maudslay and Dee believe that further education could learn from such a model because it moves away from polarities and offers students a chance to 'group and regroup' according to their needs. They are clear that they support inclusion if it genuinely expands choices for students who experience difficulties in learning. They acknowledge the inadequacy of some segregated provision and the lack of accountability that has existed in this area of work. They argue for a 'spectrum of learning support' which recognizes the individual needs of all students and meets those needs through a whole range of methodologies and patterns of learning.

SUMMARY

3.102 The overall approach to further education appears to be governed at present more by the principles of the market place than of education. The very individualistic nature of the current system of funding reinforces a notion of individual deficit and does not allow colleges to use additional support funding in a way which develops overall teaching strategies to enhance the learning of all the students in the group. The Tomlinson Committee's report is not underpinned by law. We have yet to see how many of its recommendations will be enshrined in legislation and how far a climate of inclusion can be created within the current system. You might like to think about whose interests you believe are served by criteria which can be seen to encompass the needs and aptitudes of some but not all, and whether you would like to consider other possible bases for funding.

4 TRAINING AND EMPLOYMENT

4.1 In the area of training and employment, equality of access for all is a very serious issue. As in all aspects of further and higher education, questions of funding play a very influential part in what is made available to whom. In this section we look first at the role of Training and Enterprise Councils (TECs) in providing employment-related training for young people and adults, and go on to examine services for adults provided by Social Services and local authorities.

TRAINING AND ENTERPRISE COUNCILS

4.2 The TECs are regional organizations which receive central government money to administer vocational training for school leavers and older people in their region. In England and Wales the TECs have an Operating or Licensing Agreement with the Secretaries of State for Education and Employment and for Trade and Industry to make appropriate provision within their geographic area. The TECs do not deliver the training themselves but contract it out to independent bodies which may be FE colleges, LEAs, voluntary organizations and private commercial organizations. The training is strictly vocational, contains a substantial proportion of work experience and is accredited by NVQs. In Scotland the providers' contracts are with local enterprise companies (or LECs) who in turn are contracted either by Scottish Enterprise or Highlands and Islands Enterprise.

4.3 Historically TECs were funded through the 'trainee weeks system'. This meant that, except for trainees with employed status, training providers and TECs are funded per trainee week on the basis of attendance monitoring for trainees on a daily basis. 'The Government wishes to reward providers for the retention of learners, and to ensure that public funding in respect of learners who leave their programmes early is withdrawn promptly.' (DfEE, 1996b, p. 11).

4.4 In 1996, government funding for TECs was differentiated by level of qualification. Successful achievement of an NVQ level 3 attracts a higher output payment than NVQ level 2. Most TECs were paid between 25 per cent and 40 per cent of their total Youth Training and Modern Apprenticeship budget on the basis of NVQs achieved. A small number of TECs are being paid 75 per cent of their total budget for outputs on a pilot basis. Inevitably this meant that providers tended to favour trainees likely to gain an outcome in the shortest possible time, a system likely to disadvantage people with disabilities. Although TECs are autonomous training bodies, they are expected to conform to national policies laid down by the Secretaries of State. These include being expected to make some provision for people with disabilities. Some TECs have chosen to put some of their resources into specialist schemes for people with learning difficulties. This means that they may meet their targets in terms of numbers of disabled trainees but they will be penalized in terms of outcome-related funding. Disabled trainees in residential centres are not funded by TECs but by a separate unit of the DfEE. This funding is more sensitive to the needs of trainees with disabilities and is not outcome-related.

4.5 In 1995, there were 280,000 young people in youth training schemes funded by TECs. However, there is doubt about the quality of the training offered by youth training, which has a completion rate of 46 per cent, does not require any extension of general education or formal commitment to regular attendance, punctuality, or reliability of personal organization skills, and is associated with schemes for the unemployed (Dearing, 1996, paras 5.11–3).

4.6 The Dearing review recommended the relaunch of youth training as a system of national traineeships, providing a vocational progression route to modern apprenticeships and work. Modern apprenticeships are designed to cover Level 3 of NVQs for 16+ year olds. Funding for up to 60,000 modern apprenticeships was available in 1996/7 – 5 per cent of all 16–7 year olds. There are concerns associated with equality of opportunity here. Prototype apprenticeships were in traditional male business sectors, so the preponderance of participants on modern apprenticeships has been male. The level of participation from ethnic minorities is also low.

Activity 9 Students' expectations of life after school

What do young people themselves think of provision for 16–19 year olds? What is their experience of the transition from school to work or from school to unemployment or from school to training schemes?

Now read 'From school to schemes: out of education into training' by Robert Hollands, which is Reader 1, Chapter 21.

As you read, make some notes in answer to the following questions:

- How far do the young people interviewed by Robert Hollands see their secondary schooling as a relevant preparation for their adult lives?
- What role does training play in their transition to adult life and how far is it related to expectations of securing open employment?

4.7 Robert Hollands observes that actual choices for these working-class young people were strictly limited and their opportunities seemed few. They tended to blame themselves for low achievement. Not all of them felt ready for a college course. Hollands stresses that most of them still expected to find a job on leaving school. When this proved impossible, they settled for training. He recognizes that race, gender and disability influence choice and that some young people experience more discrimination than others. He shows that choosing to go into a training programme is not a first option but a necessity. Careers officers guide young people into youth training rather than jobs.

4.8   The young people who talked to Hollands had left school with a negative self-image. They had experienced stress and failure and came to see school as irrelevant to the 'real world' of work, home and community. Work-oriented courses were seen as a deceitful and patronizing way to provide for teenagers in school, a holding on to childhood rather than a moving on to adulthood. You might like to reflect on the similarities between these young people's experiences of school and those of the Scottish girls who talked to Gwynedd Lloyd (see Unit 11/12 and Reader 1, Chapter 19).

4.9   These young people had very little freedom of choice. They would probably not benefit from staying on at school after sixteen, they were not eligible for educational grants, which do not exist for further education as they do for universities, and even a college course was unlikely because of their lack of qualifications, financial support and other social difficulties. Youth training schemes have become virtually the only option and they are now presented by careers officers as career opportunities.

4.10   The expectations of most of the young people that they would get a job on leaving school were soon dispelled and they accepted training instead. If school-based and college- or community-based vocational courses in fact lead young people nowhere near a job on completion, then what function do they have in the lives of the trainees? Should school and college curricula be reformed to reflect a different kind of relevance, encouraging a more creative and critical approach to making the transition from school to life after school? How can young people prepare themselves for the 'real world' of the 1990s?

4.11   In 1991, Jenny Corbett investigated several training programmes in different parts of the UK for the Further Education Unit (Corbett, 1991). The young people interviewed expressed similar views to those who talked to Hollands. Their parents criticised training courses for being slave labour, although some of them welcomed the extra income that came with the allowance of £35 a week. Some trainees felt that the skills they learned were of a very low level, whereas others felt that training was a genuine career opportunity. Nearly all of the trainees wanted to remain as close to home as possible.

4.12   The trainees interviewed were on youth or employment training schemes. The latter were established from 1989 for the long-term unemployed aged over eighteen. Under the influence of the TECs, any of the programmes which accommodated trainees with disabilities or learning difficulties were the first to be closed down in 1991. As Phillips (1991) reflects, the TECs cut the special needs training schemes as they were the most expensive and TECs are run by business people who are more preoccupied with profitable outcomes than offering opportunities to the long-term unemployed.

SOCIAL SERVICES

4.13   For some students, social services day centres are the only option available outside the home. These were previously known as adult training centres and are now more often referred to as social education centres. The change in name is significant in that it reflects a shift from 'keeping people occupied' towards training courses with set targets from which trainees can progress on to other courses (see the discussion of Schedule 2(j) above, p. 22). Education and training are seen as an increasingly important part of provision co-ordinated by Social Services. This is often funded by the FEFC and delivered by local FE colleges who may set up classes within a social services centre or in other cases provide classes at the college which people attend with the support of social services staff. Similarly, the care and leisure activities traditionally provided within such centres are now more often taking place in the 'community' and day centres are becoming bases from which people are supported in a whole range of mainstream activities. This has been happening for a mixture of reasons, partly philosophical and partly the result of pressure for places and cuts in Social Services budget. Cuts in budgets can mean that relationships can change from one of inter-agency collaboration to 'passing the buck'

LOCAL AUTHORITY PROVISION: ADULT EDUCATION

4.14   FE colleges do not stop educating people at the age of 18. On the contrary, the majority of students are over this age. 'Adult education', as opposed to education for adults, tends to cover areas which are non-vocational and non-accredited, such as leisure and learning for pleasure. This provision is not covered by the FEFC funding mechanisms and has been drastically reduced in recent years. However, many boroughs and LEAs maintain at least a rudimentary set of courses. Such provision is often a lifeline for people who experience difficulties in learning as it enables them to attend classes in subject areas of their choice within a mainstream community setting. If one is to see education as enhancing quality of life rather than achieving purely economic and vocational aims, it is crucial that it continues.

TRAINING AND EMPLOYMENT SCHEMES

4.15   Recently there has been an increasing emphasis on providing vocational programmes for disabled people. This trend has both positive and negative consequences.

4.16   On the positive side, FE colleges can play a very important role in enabling people with disabilities to retrain in new vocational areas. This is particularly relevant for people who may have acquired their disability later in life. In recent years such training and retraining has been enormously enhanced by the development of new technology. There are several instances of colleges which provide training in information technology using a range of specialist adaptations for people with perceptual impairments or physical disabilities thus opening up new career pathways for people who have become unemployed or have to change jobs because of their acquired disability.

4.17   Other courses for adults include training cafes and gardening schemes, and may have several funding sources, for example the voluntary sector and the European Social Fund. Such schemes can identify potential employment skills and provide supported yet real work which allows people to develop these skills.

4.18   However, on the negative side, a disappointingly small number of participants in these schemes actually progress to full-time paid employment. There may be several reasons for this:

- The short-term nature of the funding may fail to meet the long-term nature of training needs.
- Wages can often pay less than disability benefits. Disabled people are often offered low-paid work and cannot take up the offer without accepting a cut in income. Once benefit has been withdrawn, it is very difficult to get it reinstated. This situation is made worse by changing patterns of employment and the move towards part-time hours and short-term contracts.
- The unemployment rate generally remains very high.
- There is still widespread prejudice among employers about employing disabled people.

CASE STUDY – THE 'UNLOCKING EMPLOYMENT' PROJECT

4.19   'Unlocking Employment' is a European-funded project jointly managed by Kingsway College of Further Education and 'Workshop', a voluntary organization in Camden for people with learning difficulties. The project was set up to try to break the chain of people with learning difficulties moving from course to course but never actually gaining employment. Evidence suggested that not only were the numbers who gained employment very small but also that those who did find a job were not always able to sustain it. The project co-ordinator had three main areas of work – working directly with trainees, working with employers and working with families.

4.20   Direct work with trainees involved organizing training in a variety of vocational areas – particularly catering, gardening and office skills, working with both small groups and individuals on generic skills – particularly social and personal skills, communication, travel training and

Trainees in the 'Unlocking Employment' scheme

Job preparation group

Job support group.

Support for individuals.

The retail trade.

Catering.

Office skills.

time-keeping, matching individuals to jobs and working with them on interview practice, and providing continuing support when people gained employment, both on an individual basis and by running a weekly evening workshop in which participants who had gained work could discuss achievements and difficulties.

4.21   Working with employers involved alerting them to the potential of people who experience difficulties in learning, helping them to make any necessary adaptations in the workplace and maintaining ongoing contact, once a person experiencing a difficulty had been employed, to provide advice and support.

4.22   Working with families included helping, where appropriate, to prepare families for the period of transition and inevitable change that employment may bring and advising on welfare and benefit issues.

4.23   Over the three years it has been running the project has worked with over 60 people who experience difficulties in learning. Several have gained full-time employment, others work on a part-time basis, while a further group are involved in voluntary work or in extended work experience placements which may well in time lead to paid employment.

4.24   In a recent external evaluation the project was measured not just against the number of people coming off benefit and moving into work but also by looking at the extent to which people on the project experienced an improved quality of life and greater independence. In-depth interviews with trainees confirmed that even those who were not in full-time employment exhibited greatly improved levels of self-esteem and self-confidence. Another measure of success was the number of people who, while not gaining full-time employment, no longer needed to rely on day-care establishments for support.

ACCESS TO EMPLOYMENT

4.25   Recent government legislation has made some attempts to facilitate the employment of people with disabilities through the 'Access to Work' scheme. This is a scheme whereby disabled people who gain employment can receive additional resources to facilitate them taking up their post. This can take the form of specialist equipment, modification of materials, additional personnel for example a reader, initial support with induction to the job.

4.26   While this is a positive move which has benefited several disabled employees, the scheme is not without its drawbacks. Employers are often totally unaware that these funds are available, the money is not easy to access and there usually needs to be some intermediary who is familiar with the scheme and can spend time organizing the process. The legislation keeps changing and the scheme has recently suffered considerable cuts (see the *TES*, 26 January 1996).

SUMMARY

4.27 There is considerable inequity in the area the area of training and employment schemes for young people and adults. The majority of employment-related training for school-leavers and for adults is administered by regional TECs funded through central government. The output-related funding mechanism may disadvantage disabled trainees who need longer to achieve their targets, despite the advantages of the additional resources available to them. The quality of some youth training schemes contracted through TECs is doubtful. Non-vocational adult education organized by LEAs which does not meet the FEFC criteria for funding has been drastically reduced.

5 HIGHER EDUCATION

5.1 In this section we investigate recent initiatives in widening access to higher education, and examine how far disability, gender and class are associated with lower levels of participation and inequality of opportunity for some students.

WIDENING ACCESS

5.2 More occupations are now seeking professional status and more professions are seeking graduate entrants. Total undergraduate numbers increased from 1983/4 to 1993/4 by nearly 80 per cent, of which 54 per cent was between 1989 and 1994.

5.3 In July 1992, the Higher Education Funding Council (HEFC) established an Advisory Group on Access and Participation (AGAP) to advise the Council on ways to encourage diversity in higher education, widen access and increase opportunities. AGAP developed three special initiatives for the Council:

- in 1993/4, £0.5 million was allocated to 17 institutions to increase the participation of students from ethnic minorities in initial teacher training;
- in 1993/4, £3 million was allocated to 38 institutions to widen access for students with special needs;
- in 1994/5, £3 million was allocated to 48 institutions for a further initiative to widen access to students with special needs

  (Cusack, 1996)

5.4 The initiatives' purpose was to increase participation from two groups: students from ethnic minorities and students 'with special needs'. The Teacher Training Authority (TTA) has now taken over responsibility for increasing the participation of minority groups in initial teacher training.

5.5 In the early 1990s, many of the new universities (i.e. the ex-polytechnics and ex-DfE-funded institutions) took steps to improve access and encourage disabled applicants. Several of them have appointed disability co-ordinators and created a 'named person' who is responsible for managing liaison with disabled students. People in these posts work in a variety of ways – individual counselling support, training of other staff, awareness-raising among students, etc. However, it is unusual for hours to be allocated for individual on-going support as it is in FE.

5.6 Widening access is a common theme in many institutions' mission statements and strategic plans. Statements vary from explicit policies and intentions to more general assumptions, but few institutions have translated this desire into targeted activity. Old universities are likely to have greater difficulty in developing institution-wide admissions policies with specific access-related goals. This 'may reflect different traditions of leadership and management' (Cusack, 1996, p. 27). Institutions with a clearly defined strategic access policy have significantly contributed to increasing the diversity of the student population. Examples of specific action include:

- flexible approaches to admissions which take account of non-traditional entry qualifications and students' prior experiences;
- links: outreach, associated student schemes and other links with schools, employers and particular communities;
- collaborative arrangements both with FE colleges through franchise and associate college arrangements and with Open College Networks to facilitate entry routes to HE.

5.7 Examples of indirect action which contributes to wider access as part of a broader purpose include:

- modularization: both modular and credit frameworks provide opportunities for greater flexibility in mode and pattern of study for non-traditional students in particular;
- open learning: developments in IT and multi-media have opened up possibilities for innovation in the delivery of teaching and learning within institutions and off-campus.

5.8 The recent expansion in numbers has itself created a more diverse student population. The number of students entering higher education with non-standard qualifications is already significant and likely to increase. A broader student profile exists in the new universities. This may reflect clearly defined strategic access policies which widen admission using both direct action through specific admissions policies and partnerships with FE colleges, employers and particular communities, and indirect action through modular courses and open learning. Part-time students, for example, tend to have different qualifications and HE experience from those of full-time students. In the future many more young entrants to HE may have qualifications other than A-levels. Dearing (1995) suggested that A level courses are suited to only one third of 18 year olds. Vocational qualifications are likely therefore to become an increasingly important entry route to HE.

5.9 The development of the new universities and the growth in student numbers (particularly the increase in mature students) has led to a more student centred approach to learning. Methods of course delivery and design are being developed to incorporate a range of styles and alternative assessment procedures devised to help all students, especially those coming into HE a long time after the end of compulsory schooling.

5.10 Opportunities for female students have improved considerably in recent years. Women now represent approximately half of all HE students. However, there are still few women taking courses in engineering, technology, mathematical sciences, it and computing, and built environment. The proportion of men is lower than women in subjects and professions allied to medicine and education.

5.11 There are also interesting differences of representation among ethnic minority groups:

- A higher proportion of black and Asian students pursue part-time courses than other ethnic minorities.

- Black students are mostly over 21 in both full- and part-time courses.

- There are proportionately more male Bangladeshi and Pakistani students and more female students among other minority ethnic groups.

- Over 60 per cent of all ethnic minority students are in the ex-polytechnics and ex-DfEE institutions. The proportion of students from Asian groups at former universities is as high, or higher than, for the population as a whole; the proportion of black students is significantly lower.

  (Cusack, 1996)

5.12 However, there is also a serious question of under-representation in two areas: children of non-managerial/professional parents, and disabled students. Children of professional and managerial classes continue to predominate. In 1963, the Robbins Report on higher education found, like previous reports, a high correlation between social class and educational attainment – a child, for example, of professional parents was 20 times more likely to enter full-time higher education than the child of semi-skilled and unskilled workers (Great Britain, 1963). But once admitted to university, working-class students performed as well as middle-class. Robbins concluded that there was a huge untapped 'pool of ability' in the population, and recommended a massive expansion in higher education.

Currently no relevant national data exist on the socio-economic composition of the over-21-year-old student body. However, among the under-21 group of full-time students in higher education, the professional, managerial and associated social classes represent over 60 per cent of undergraduates, yet only 37 per cent of all economically active people. Most students from professional backgrounds are in the old universities; most from non-managerial and technical backgrounds in the ex-polytechnics and ex-DfE-funded institutions. People from less advantaged groups also tend to enter higher education later in life. Information from the Universities and Colleges Admissions Service (1994) shows that 47 per cent of entrants aged 21 to 24 came from non-managerial or professional backgrounds, compared with 35 per cent aged under 19.

5.13   Students with disabilities make up a very small proportion of those in higher education. It appears that students with certain disabilities are less well able to access higher education than others. This might reflect the severity of the disability and/or the level of resourcing required to support particular students. There are nearly 27 000 undergraduates known to have a disability, approximately 2 per cent of the student body. The greatest numbers either have dyslexia or report themselves to have an 'unseen' disability. Overall, 68 per cent of disabled students are full-time, but students with mobility difficulties, multiple disabilities and those reported to have 'mental health problems' are predominantly part-time.

5.14   The Open University is an important provider for disabled students in general and still offers the most extensive services. This provision includes weekend residential courses to prepare students with visual and hearing impairments for university study, the use of interpreters and assistants at summer schools, and the loan and maintenance of high quality technical equipment for home use. It also involves specialist support and guidance in study skills and help for those students who have difficulty in reading and writing for their assignments. Course units are routinely read on to audio-cassettes for blind students.

5.15   Students at higher education institutions are entitled to a grant from their home LEA to meet support costs. This could include technical equipment, personal care support, additional transport costs or communicators. While this is a positive move there are certain drawbacks. The onus to co-ordinate this support (if it is not provided from within the institution) is on the student and accessing it can be complex. Further, the budget does not always cover all a student's requirements.

5.16   Despite the increase in undergraduate numbers over the past few years, university education in the UK still remains highly selective. Drop-out rates from higher education in 1996 stood at around 13 per cent. 'Anecdotal evidence suggests that non-traditional students (older people entering university without necessarily having followed the A-level route) are more likely to withdraw. The reasons may relate to a range of factors – financial, academic or pastoral ...' (Cusack, 1996, p.31). The financial burden on students and their families is increasing as student grants are frozen and loans increase. Many more students are experiencing financial hardship with more full-time students having to supplement their finances. The rise in student hardship and indebtedness may produce significant barriers to future participation for non-traditional students in future. Increasing student numbers combined with financial restraints have resulted in students having far less direct contact time with staff, and many of them, particularly those who have come from the supportive context of an access programme in FE, may find it hard to adapt to the degree of self-directed study required. Also, despite the developments in course delivery, many universities (particularly the 'old' ones) still run courses which discriminate in favour of those who have followed the traditional A-level path and not those who have come through the Access or BTEC/GNVQ route.

SUMMARY

5.17 Although more students now progress to HE, most do not. Changes in HE have not all been in the direction of improving access for all. Some disabled students move on to HE, although these still remain a small minority. The number of students with non-professional or non-managerial parents is still proportionately low. Drop-out rates among older students who entered university through a non-traditional route are proportionately high.

6 CONCLUSION

EQUALITY OF OPPORTUNITY FOR ALL?

6.1 As you reflect on what you have read in this unit, how far do you feel there is equality of opportunity for everyone in further and higher education and on schemes related to employment? Do you think it is possible to guarantee the resources needed to include those who are marginalized socially, economically and occupationally or who may have a disability? How do you consider the current situation reflects the value placed on individuals in our society?

6.2 Government pressures are forcing FE to become more and more vocational. The current emphasis on training for employment may be seen to threaten the broadly educative function of further education, for example the curtailing of non-vocational learning for leisure and pleasure courses. There is an irony in that this is occurring at a time when, for a variety of reasons, people are increasingly likely to experience periods of unemployment in their lives. It is also less and less likely that people will stay within one vocational area throughout their working lives and so they will increasingly require a range of transferable knowledge and skills. We began this discussion by looking at the concept of adult status and demonstrating that while work is an important indicator of this status it is not the only one. The reality is that despite attempts to support disabled people in employment, the majority remain unemployed. Research carried out between 1989 and 1991 in Scotland (Ward et al., 1994) followed 618 school leavers 'with special educational needs' and found, two years later, that only 9 per cent were in full-time employment. One conclusion of the Scottish survey was that educational and training programmes for this group could mask the true levels of unemployment. This is true not only of people who are registered disabled but also for those whose difficulties in learning have been created by the social and educational environment. For many within this group, life can become a continuous cycle of courses and training programmes which never lead to real employment. There is a conundrum here: on the one hand, is it fair to have students continually working towards employment when they may well never achieve it, and, on the other, is it right to deny anyone employment or the opportunity of a *real* job?

6.3 The purpose of education for any group of individuals may change at different stages of their life according to their age, whether they are in a job, their living situation or personal aspirations and interests. The challenge for further and higher education is to make provision which is flexible enough to meet this range of needs and to support individuals in leading fulfilled adult lives. We have argued that the concept of adult status can change according to its economic, social and cultural context. What does not change is the importance of recognizing education as something which should enhance the quality of life and open up the possibility of individuals achieving their own aspirations. As Tomlinson (1996) points out, currently there are groups of adults who may have experienced some sort of difficulty in learning who have had very little access to education. As children, they may have been excluded from education altogether or segregated into special provision. Others who experienced similar difficulties in learning but who are younger may have been educated in mainstream schools with or without additional support for their learning. All the more reason, then, for opening up more educational opportunities for adults who were denied access in the past. One of the challenges for educators, particularly in meeting the needs of people who experience difficulties in learning, or who have disabilities, is to find more effective ways to discover what their aspirations are and to establish the means by which people can access the necessary resources to achieve those aspirations as of right.

6.4 As in other areas of non-statutory provision, how money is allocated exerts a strong influence over equality of access to schemes related to employment and training. Where funding is tied to output, some trainees will be more attractive to course providers than others. TECs do not have much incentive to attempt to make provision for some trainees who need particular kinds of support. A greater percentage of performance-related funding is allocated for an outcome achieved by someone with a disability, but this tends to be counteracted by the increasing percentage of funding which is linked to outcomes that are actually achieved.

6.5   In HE, there has been a rapid increase in undergraduate numbers, but the result of changes has not always been increased access for all. Children of non-managerial or non-professional parents and disabled students, in particular those with limited mobility or multiple disabilities, are still under-represented in proportion to other students. In addition, older students entering university through non-traditional routes are more likely to withdraw from HE for a variety of factors which may be financial, academic or pastoral.

6.6   The question of how far there is real equality of opportunity in further and higher education and in employment-related training schemes may be answered in part by looking at some of the results of the 1989–91 survey undertaken in Scotland, mentioned above. This showed that the pathway for individuals with 'records', the Scottish equivalent of statements, was related to the type of difficulty identified on the record. Where a physical/sensory difficulty was recorded, students usually remained at school and then went on to possible professional employment. Students assessed as having 'mild/moderate learning difficulties' usually left school to undertake work training/experience, after which their future was often unknown, while students assessed as having 'severe learning difficulties' tended to remain in a residential institution, and their futures were also unknown. Where 'social, emotional-behavioural problems' were on students' records, they usually became unemployed on leaving school, but subsequently might obtain low-level employment.

6.7   You may well conclude that where a disability or difficulty appears to be so closely associated with future life chances, any one individual has very little freedom of choice and very little value is placed on him or her. As Fish observes:

> In many instances expectations have been too low ... Recent developments have shown that appropriate education, training and direct experience of work and living away from home, can enable a very significant proportion of those with severe disabilities to maintain themselves in employment and independent life.

(Reader 2, p. 129)

6.8   If this is the case, there is little reason other than money why this education and training should not be provided so that everyone might participate more fully in the mainstream of society. Decisions about whose needs to finance may be seen as largely a question of whom we value. Perhaps in the end access to a whole range of resources in FE will have to be underpinned by the law if we are to reduce some of the current inequalities.

6.9   Resources intended to facilitate access to education, training or employment and offered as a concession may be withdrawn when no longer considered a priority. Resources given as of legal right, on the other hand, can offer a guarantee.

7 INVESTIGATIONS

VIEWS ON INCLUSION

7.1 Interview a small group of three or four students who have moved into further or higher education from a special school. The aim is to explore their perceptions and experiences in the light of their past compulsory schooling. Each interview should last no more than thirty minutes. You should ask your interviewees:

(a) to describe how they came to be in further/higher education;

(b) to discuss their choice of course and the subject areas they are pursuing;

(c) to discuss their school experience and contrast it with FE or HE experience;

(d) to describe any changes in practice they would like to see;

(e) to consider what move they would like to make next and why.

Remember: you may have to pay particular attention to how you phrase these questions and how you elicit a response.

POLICY FOR EQUAL OPPORTUNITIES

7.2 Investigate the extent to which a college policy for equal opportunities might or might not include issues of learning difficulties and disabilities. Interview two staff about these issues, including the learning support co-ordinator at the college. You should find out:

(a) what written policy documents exist in the college and the extent to which the learning support co-ordinator was involved in helping to draft them;

(b) which issues are addressed by the policy;

(c) what steps have been taken to implement this policy;

(d) what difficulties have arisen during the implementation of the policy;

(e) the extent to which curriculum development is addressed in the policy;

(f) the extent to which the Disability Discrimination Act has influenced the policy and its implementation (see Unit 14/15 for a discussion of the Act).

TRANSITION IN THE CODE OF PRACTICE

7.3 Investigate the extent to which the Code of Practice transition section has influenced practice in mainstream or special schools or colleges of further education. Talk to two or three teachers from one such institution. They might be learning support tutors or subject tutors in comprehensive schools, special schools or colleges. Each interview should last no more than thirty minutes. You should ask the interviewees:

(a) has the Code led to improved transition arrangements between school and college in their experience?

(b) what difficulties have they experienced in implementing the Code?

(c) what changes in policy and/or practice would help implementation?

(d) have the changes in transition arrangements broadened or narrowed the choices for this student group?

APPENDIX 1   THE TRANSITION SECTION IN THE CODE OF PRACTICE

Annual reviews from age 14–19

6:42. Some pupils with statements of special educational needs will remain in school after the age of 16. LEAs remain responsible for such pupils until they are 19. Others with statements will, however, leave school at 16, moving, for example, to a college within the further education sector or to social services provision. But, whatever the intended future destination of the young person, the annual review has an additional significance as he or she approaches the age of 16.

6:43. The first annual review after the young person's 14th birthday should involve the agencies who will play a major role during the post-school years. The transfer of relevant information should ensure that young people receive any necessary specialist help or support during their continuing education and vocational or occupational training after leaving school. For young people with disabilities, the role of social services departments will be of particular importance and local authorities have specific duties relating to other legislation which are set out below.

The first annual review after the young person's fourteenth birthday

6:44. The annual review procedure described above applies with the following exceptions:

- **the LEA convene the review meeting, even when the young person is at school. The LEA must invite the child's parents and relevant member of staff, any people specified by the head teacher, and anyone else the LEA consider appropriate**
- **the LEA must also ensure that other providers, such as social services, are aware of the annual review and the procedures to be followed, and must invite the social services department to attend the review so that any parallel assessments under the Disabled Persons Act (1986); the NHS and Community Care Act 1990; and the Chronically Sick and Disabled Persons Act 1970 can contribute to and draw information from the review process**

- the LEA must invite the careers service to be represented at the review meeting, to enable all options for further education, careers and occupational training to be given serious consideration. The careers service will also be able to identify any specific targets which should be set as part of the annual review to ensure that independence training, personal and social skills, and other aspects of the wider curriculum are fully addressed during the young person's last years at school

- the LEA prepare the review report and the Transition Plan after the meeting, and circulate these to the young person's parents, the head teacher, all those from whom advice was sought, all those attending the review meeting and any others the LEA consider appropriate. In particular, the LEA should consider passing the review report and Transition Plan to the FEFC, particularly in cases where a decision might need to be taken about specialist college provision outside the further education sector (see also paragraphs 6:56–6:58).

The Transition Plan

6:45. The first annual review after the young person's 14th birthday and any subsequent annual reviews until the child leaves school should include a **Transition Plan** which will draw together information from a range of individuals within and beyond the school in order to plan coherently for the young person's transition to adult life. Under sections 5 and 6 of the Disabled Persons Act 1986, at the first annual review after a child's 14th birthday LEAs must seek information from social services departments as to whether a child with a statement under Part III of the Education Act 1993 is disabled and may require services from the local authority when leaving school. LEAs should also consult child health services and any other professionals such as educational psychologists, therapists or occupational psychologists who may have a useful contribution to make.

6:46. The Transition Plan should address the following questions:

The School

- What are the young person's curriculum needs during transition? How can the curriculum help the young person to play his or her role in the community; make use of leisure and recreational facilities; assume new roles in the family; develop new educational and vocational skills?

The Professionals

- How can they develop close working relationships with colleagues in other agencies to ensure effective and coherent plans for the young person in transition?
- Which new professionals need to be involved in planning for transition, for example occupational psychologists; a rehabilitation medicine specialist; occupational and other therapists?
- Does the young person have any special health or welfare needs which will require planning and support from health and social services now or in the future?
- Are assessment arrangements for transition clear, relevant and shared between all agencies concerned?
- How can information best be transferred from children's to adult services to ensure a smooth transitional arrangement?
- Where a young person requires a particular technological aid, do the arrangements for transition include appropriate training and arrangements for securing technological support?
- Is education after the age of 16 appropriate, and if so, at school or at a college of further education?

The Family

- What do parents expect of their son's or daughter's adult life?
- What can they contribute in terms of helping their child develop personal and social skills, an adult life-style and acquire new skills?
- Will parents experience new care needs and require practical help in terms of aids, adaptations or general support during these years?

The Young Person

- What information do young people need in order to make informed choices?
- What local arrangements exist to provide advocacy and advice if required?
- How can young people be encouraged to contribute to their own Transition Plan and make positive decisions about the future?
- If young people are living away from home or attending a residential school outside their own LEA, are there special issues relating to the location of services when they leave school which should be discussed in planning?
- What are the young person's hopes and aspirations for the future, and how can these be met?

6:47. The Transition Plan should build on the conclusions reached and targets set at previous annual reviews, including the contributions of teachers responsible for careers education and guidance. It should focus on strengths as well as weaknesses and cover all aspects of the young person's development, allocating clear responsibility for different aspects of development to specific agencies and professionals. LEAs should advise schools on the proper balance of the transition programme components and ensure that all relevant information is available, together with advice and support as required. Social services departments, the health services and the careers service should be actively involved in the plan.

Involvement of social services departments

6:48. The first annual review after a child's 14th birthday will have a special significance because of the LEA's duties under sections 5 and 6 of the Disabled Persons (Services, Consultation and Representation) Act 1986. Sections 5 and 6 of that Act require LEAs to seek information from social services departments as to whether a child with a statement under Part III of the Education Act 1993 is disabled and may require services from the local authority when leaving school. The LEA must inform the appropriate and designated officer of the relevant social services department of the date of the child's first annual review after his or her 14th birthday and must similarly inform the social services department (if it is agreed that the child in question is disabled) between eight and 12 months before the expected school leaving date. LEAs may also inform social services departments at any time *after* the particular annual review required under section 5 of the Disabled Persons Act if it is considered that circumstances have changed and the young person concerned may now be considered to be disabled.

6:49. LEAs and, so far as is reasonable, schools should familiarise themselves with the following Acts, which may directly affect the future provision available to a young person with special educational needs:

The Chronically Sick and Disabled Persons Act 1970

The Employment and Training Act 1973 as amended by the Trade Union Reform and Employment Rights Act 1993

The Disabled Persons (Services, Consultation and Representation) Act 1986

The Children Act 1989

The National Health Service and Community Care Act 1990

The Further and Higher Education Act 1992

6:50. Under the Children Act 1989 and the NHS and Community Care Act 1990, social services departments are required to arrange a multi-disciplinary assessment and provide care plans for children and adults with significant special needs – which may include the provision of further education facilities.

6:51. The transition period may be associated with increasing levels of disability in some young people. It may therefore be necessary to plan for future increased special needs and for the provision of aids and adaptations both in a home and an educational setting. Young people may choose **not** to be assessed as disabled under sections 5 and 6 of the Disabled Persons Act and may similarly choose **not** to request help through the local authority community care arrangements. The LEA should give details of any relevant voluntary organisation or professional agency providing advice and counselling if such advice is needed. Schools should have information available on local sources of help and advice, including any local disability organisations which can provide information on the wider range of local services and offer independent advice and advocacy if required.

6:52. Local authority social services departments have duties under Section 24 of the Children Act 1989 to make arrangements for young people over 18 who are regarded as being 'in need' and who have been looked after by the local authority or received services from them prior to that date. LEAs should therefore ensure that the young person is aware of the power of the social services department to provide assistance beyond the age of 18 and provide any relevant information to the social services department in question in order to alert them of any potential special needs. Where a young person has been looked after in a foster placement or a residential home or attended a residential school outside his or her own local authority, the LEA should seek to ensure liaison between all relevant LEAs and social services departments.

The role of the careers service

6:53. The careers service must be invited to the first annual review following the young person's 14th birthday, and should also be invited to all subsequent annual reviews. Vocational guidance should be presented in the wider context of information on further education and training courses and should take fully into account the wishes and feelings of the young person concerned. The careers officer with specialist responsibilities should provide continuing oversight of, and information on, the young person's choice of provision, and assist the LEA and school in securing such provision and providing advice, counselling and support as appropriate. In some circumstances careers officers may also wish to involve occupational psychologists, who can contribute to the development of a vocational profile of a young person for whom future planning is giving cause for concern. Schools may in particular welcome guidance on curriculum development in independence, social or other skills, and ways of involving young people themselves in assessment and in strategies to address any behavioural or other problems which may otherwise adversely affect their further education or future employment.

6:54. Records of Achievement should be used, with the young person's consent, to provide information to colleges or any other provision to which the young person may move on leaving school. Where appropriate, Records of Achievement can be produced in Braille as well as in print, can make use of pictorial or abstract symbol systems, and may include a range of illustrative material (including supporting photographs, tapes or videos) which provide information on the young person.

Information

6:55. Circular 93/05 (B19/93 in Wales) from the Further Education Funding Council contains advice on the Council's arrangements for funding placements for students with learning difficulties and disabilities. It is the FEFC's responsibility in such circumstances to ensure that an assessment is made when such young people enter further education; in practice the LEA conducts the assessment on the FEFC's behalf in many cases. Circular 93/05 states that the assessment should be based upon:

- **the availability to young people and their advocates of a full range of information from the LEA about post-16 education and training choices, to inform placement decisions as indicated in the Parent's Charter**
- **the involvement of young people, their parents and their advocates in the assessment process, and**
- **the advice, wherever possible, of a range of professionals to ensure expert guidance, including for example careers officers, educational psychologists and other specialists who have knowledge of the individual's needs.**

Transfer to the further education sector

6:56. LEAs should ensure that where a young person has a statement of special educational needs, a copy of the statement together with a copy of the most recent annual review (together with any advice or information appended to it including the Transition Plan) should be passed to the social services department and the college or other provision that the young person will be attending. Where a decision might need to be taken by the FEFC about the placement of a student in a specialist college outside the FE sector, a copy of the Transition Plan should be sent to the FEFC. LEAs should seek the agreement of students and parents to the transfer of information (including statements) from school to the further education sector, but should explain the importance of such information and the desirability of the transfer.

6:57. Where students or their families consider that the information contained in the statement or annual review presents a negative picture or is inaccurate in some way, the LEA should consider how the review process can be made more positive and participative at the time of transition so that the conclusions of the last annual review are seen as an action plan for future development. The LEA should consider including in the review report information such as Records of Achievement which present the student in a positive light and provide information about his or her wider interests and abilities. The LEA should seek the consent of parents and students prior to the final annual review for the transfer of the review report and any Records of Achievement to the FEFC.

6:58. Schools should foster links with local further education colleges. This will help in the decision-making process and in the eventual transition itself, easing the move for both young person and staff at the further education college. Link provision with colleges can be of particular benefit to a young person with special educational needs by providing opportunities for integration, extending the curriculum and offering an induction into the adult environment of further education.

The involvement of young people in assessment and review

6:59. The views of young people themselves should be sought and recorded wherever possible in any assessment, reassessment or review during the years of transition. Some young people may wish to express these views through a trusted professional, family, independent advocate or adviser, the Named Person or through an officer of the authority. Effective arrangements for transition will involve young people themselves addressing issues of:

- **personal development**
- **self-advocacy**
- **the development of a positive self-image**
- **awareness of the implications of any long-term health problem or disability and**
- **the growth of personal autonomy and the acquisition of independent living skills.**

6:60. If the growth of these personal skills is to complement the student's progress through agreed academic and vocational curriculum arrangements and to inform choices about continuing education and future employment, student involvement on a regular basis in the annual review process should be encouraged.

Encouraging student involvement in decision-making during transition:

- **schools and LEAs should consider ways of ensuring that students' views are incorporated in planning for transition – for example the use of student counsellors, advocates or advisers, the Named Person, social workers or peer support**

- curriculum planning should focus on activities which encourage students to review and reflect upon their own experiences and wishes and to formulate and articulate their views

- the student will need to come to terms with the wider implications of his or her disability or special need in adult life. Careful attention should be given to the avoidance of stigmatising language or labels and to the provision of accurate and sensitive advice and information on any aspects of the disability or special need as required

- transition should be seen as a continuum. Students should be encouraged to look to the future and plan how they will develop the academic, vocational, personal and social skills necessary to achieve their long-term objectives. Records of Achievement can demonstrate success and enable young people to recognise and value their own achievements as a contribution to their future learning and adult status and

- students will be most effectively involved in decision-making when supported by information, careers guidance, counselling, work experience and the opportunity to consider a wide range of options during the transition phase.

Students without statements but with special educational needs

6:61. In some instances, a student approaching the age of 16 may have special educational needs which do not call for a statement, but which are likely to require some support if he or she goes on to further education. To ensure that these students are able to make decisions, and to facilitate their successful transition, it is important that they have appropriate help and guidance. This might include the provision of school/college link courses or work placements and should involve the different local agencies concerned. Further education colleges will need a thorough assessment of the young person's needs in order to make soundly based decisions about appropriate provision.

6:62. Schools providing support to students through the school-based stages of assessment should therefore consult as appropriate with other relevant services, such as the careers service, to ensure that relevant, detailed information is transferred to the FEFC, with the young person's consent. The LEA should provide schools with information on transition to the FE sector and details of local and national voluntary organisations which may help such students and their families. In some cases, schools may wish to prepare their own transition plans for students with special educational needs, but without a statement.

Source: DEPARTMENT FOR EDUCATION (1994) *Code of Practice on the Identification and Assessment of Special Educational Needs*, London, DfE, pp. 116–23.

APPENDIX 2   THE ORGANIZATION OF 'ADDITIONAL SUPPORT' PROVISION IN FE COLLEGES

A   INTEGRATED PROVISION

Blackburn College is a vocational further education college offering National Vocational Qualifications in a range of practical subject areas including catering, hairdressing, motor mechanics, painting and decorating. Each year many students who have previously been categorized as having 'moderate' and 'severe' learning difficulties are integrated into mainstream vocational programmes.

The College offers inclusive provision for all students who experience difficulties in learning. The provision is organized through the Learning Support Manager who is based in Student Services. She works very closely with the four specialist Learning Support Organizers for Dyslexia Support, Language Support, Maths and English Support, and for Students 'with Learning Difficulties'.

Identification of Support Needs (Initial)

All full-time students identify support needs on an application form and additional information may come from schools. Information relating to those students requiring support is passed to faculties via the Learning Support Manager. Students from Special Schools are invited in for assessment days in their faculty prior to September so that support can be in place from Day One. The learning needs of part-time students are identified during a short interview.

Key Support Tutors

The role of the Key Support Tutor developed in response to the perceived needs of students who experience difficulties in learning. One tutor is assigned to each vocational area, such as hairdressing or catering and is expected to have an overview of it. It is the responsibility of the tutor to keep mainstream staff informed of the support needs of students and to ensure that individuals have a suitable curriculum. They provide some support but also teach the whole group. This may include teaching study skills or vocational skills if they have the requisite qualifications.

During the assessment period for students who experience difficulties in learning, or who have disabilities, Key Support Tutors build up a detailed picture of the whole group. As time has gone on they have become accepted as members of faculties, attend faculty staff meetings and are recognized as the initial person to approach regarding support.

Identification of Support Needs

All full-time students on Foundation or Intermediate courses take part in a screening process in the first week. This is done alongside a support tutor working in a theory session of the course in order to observe and identify any students who may require support. The in-class support tutor will then sit down with the course team to discuss the support needs of individuals within the group and the support tutor will feed that information back to the Learning Support Organizers. Individual students can refer themselves or be referred at any time. Support takes many forms and may include the following:

- support worker to assist mobility and practical support
- communicators and lip speakers for students with a hearing impairment
- tutors with expertise in working with students who experience difficulties in learning, teaching alongside mainstream staff
- extra tutorial time for students with psychological problems
- specialist help for dyslexic students
- extra support in basic English and Maths delivered through workshop provision, 1:1 support and in-class support
- back up sessions to supplement theory sessions
- help with organizational skills
- provision of specialist equipment
- staff development days to raise awareness, plan curriculum, adapt materials
- support in work placements
- home liaison
- individual action planning with the student
- oral testing of underpinning knowledge

Strengths of the approach as identified by the Learning Support Manager

1 We work towards adult status and have found that students are able to grow up more quickly when they are expected to, and observe other students behave in this way.

2 All students are part of a mainstream group and will wherever possible stay with this group although they may be working towards slightly different accreditation or at a slower pace. If necessary students can have individual timetables covering more than one area – for example on sampling programmes.

3 Attitudes and values of staff have changed enormously where they have been supported in working with students who experience difficulties in learning, or who have disabilities.

4   Students have access to workshops and work placements in the same way as other students.

5   Where students do require Independent Living Skills this is done on a 1:1 basis by support workers or sometimes by outside agencies. It is always done in a 'real' setting.

6   Mainstream tutors have accepted responsibility for students – there is nowhere else for them to go now. They have been surprised by what they have achieved and are proud of them.

7   'Special needs' tutors have been able to concentrate on supporting students in the mainstream and on working with mainstream staff.

8   It has been possible to develop material alongside mainstream tutors with both tutors working together – an effective form of staff development.

9   Students have exceeded everyone's expectations.

10 Support can be matched to individual students and is flexible. The Key Support Tutor is crucial in monitoring this.

Disadvantages as identified by the Learning Support Manager

1   It can be an administrative nightmare keeping tabs on students across the whole college. Liaison is crucial but takes a lot of time.

2   Time is needed to work with [potential students, mainly adults, who may not appreciate that college offers different experiences than it did three years ago. This is intensified by the loss of much non-vocational provision.

B   DESIGNATED PROVISION IN AN FE COLLEGE

This is a case study of a Team Enterprise project at Lewisham College for a group of students who experience severe difficulties in learning. It describes how Lewisham College adapted an initiative called Team Enterprise as the means to enrich the curriculum for some students. Team Enterprise which grew out of the Young Enterprise Award requires students to set up and run a small business for the duration of their course. The team has to decide on a product, set up a board of directors, sell shares in the company, produce, market and sell their goods. They are supported in this by the course staff and by business advisers who are drawn from the local business community. One adviser is an employee of the local Business and Education Partnership and two are from local Midland banks. The emphasis is on learning by doing and on processes as much as outcomes. Students can develop work related skills whether or not the company is actually successful.

Lewisham College is a large further education college serving south-east London. It offers an extensive range of vocational courses leading to national qualifications alongside GCSE and A-level programmes. The College runs a well established two-year general education course for students with severe cognitive disabilities which up until September 1994 was followed by a year-long further options course. The purpose of this course was to address the need for the further development of social and life skills and greater independence within the community. However, Jenny Wilson, the course tutor, felt that this final year did not adequately address the world of work. After attending the London launch of Team Enterprise which invited local schools and colleges to examine national examples of good practice and suggest how Team Enterprise could be implemented in ways which would suit the needs of designated groups of students with disabilities, the course team at Lewisham decided to adopt it as a means of extending their curriculum.

The Project

The team at Lewisham took the decision to develop a company which not only produced one or two saleable items but also offered a wide range of services associated with fresh and dried flowers. Thus in October 1994 'Pozyganza' was launched. The project has two staff, a tutor and a learning support worker, and an intake of eight students per year, usually aged between 21 and 30. Students attend for three days a week and on the remaining two days are linked into community provision near to their homes. Initially 50 per cent of the potential course hours were designated for the project but now the whole of the curriculum is delivered via the Team Enterprise framework. The company has developed from making up small personal orders for staff and students to winning contracts with the college restaurants, providing major displays for college events such as Black History Week and European Careers Day, and providing floral displays for national bodies such as the FEFC and the TUC. Both the course and the students have a very high profile within the college and in the wider community. In particular students are given access to a range of people and experiences which may otherwise have remained unknown to them. As the Project's first year report points out the situation is not one-way but strongly reciprocal as 'students have heightened the advisers awareness of disability and given them an understanding of the relevance and benefits of work to a group of disadvantaged individuals about whom it is all too easy to make negative assumptions.'

Outcomes and Progression

The company has been very successful but it is important not to lose sight of the fact that it is a course intended to develop the skills and experience of the students. The intention is not to turn out florists, although there are plans to introduce the National Proficiency Credit in floristry for those students for whom it is appropriate, but to develop in students a range of generic, transferable skills which will benefit them in any work situation and in a wider range of life situations. This is reflected in the intended learning outcomes which are clearly defined in the course literature. Students are involved in the self-assessment of these skills and this year achievement is being recorded via the Youth Award Work Right Certificate. Progression routes for students have included:

- horticultural training projects
- work in Garden Centres
- Social Services/Lifestyles employment (this is a package of education/leisure and supported employment)

Competition for supported and open employment is strong but tutors are optimistic that students will attain it because they can demonstrate tangible skills that they have learnt on the course.

Evaluation of Pozyganza

Pozyganza demonstrates some of the components which may be perceived as negative characteristics of specialist provision:

- students are taught only by specialist staff
- activity takes place largely in a designated base room
- the target group is specifically students with severe cognitive disabilities

However, it is possibly because the provision is specifically designed for this group that it has been so successful. Team Enterprise has provided a framework around which staff have been able to meet the needs and aspirations of their student group without modifying or diminishing the award itself. It is not partial achievement but sound, effective education which contextualizes learning and enables all of the students involved to contribute at an equal level. The validity of the project has been recognized by the organizational body of Team Enterprise who have highlighted it as being an example of outstanding practice. However, it is not a stand alone piece of provision but part of a range of educational programmes which Lewisham College provides for students who experience difficulties in learning, or who have disabilities,. This includes both designated and integrated provision and covers both adults and school leavers. Students may be on specially designed courses, be on mainstream programmes and receive additional support, or simply attend courses where they do not need any specific support. A 1995 FEFC Inspection report graded their overall provision for this student group as Grade One which is the highest grade, stating that provision for students who experience difficulties in learning, or who have disabilities, within the college was particularly wide and of outstanding quality.

APPENDIX 3   BEYOND THE 'INCLUSIONIST' DEBATE

Much recent discussion about provision for students with learning difficulties and disabilities has focused around the 'inclusionist debate'. …We want to … focus on two main issues. The first is to recognize the current practical limitations of including all students with learning difficulties and disabilities into mainstream provision without fundamental changes to that mainstream offer. While accepting the importance of the vision (i.e. including *all* students within the further education framework) we feel it is irresponsible to assume that this goal can be achieved within the situation as it currently exists. Secondly, we feel that the vision itself requires certain redefinitions. The debate appears to have become locked into a skewed polarity between 'integration' and 'segregation' and what we hope to postulate in the second half of this paper is a model which goes beyond this polarity and instead looks at a framework for further and adult education which allows for students with learning difficulties and disabilities to be able to follow patterns of learning which are most appropriate to their individual requirements.

THE CHANGING FURTHER AND ADULT EDUCATION CURRICULUM

The shape of the new post-16 curriculum is beginning to emerge and the change is not without difficulty. In reality many students are still taught in groups by largely didactic methods (MacFarlane, 1993) and follow one or two-year courses of study. It is still relatively rare in most colleges for students to follow individual learning plans on modular programmes using a variety of learning methods with access to appropriate learning support. The 1991 White Paper *Education and Training for the 21st Century* set down a series of national education and training targets in an attempt to improve the quality of the workforce and bring the UK into line with standards in the rest of the developed world. New controls over the curriculum offer were introduced by funding only certain kinds of programmes.

The impact of many of these changes remains to be seen. There is a fear however that, combined with a squeeze on resources, schools and colleges will compete for those students with higher levels of attainment who are likely to complete courses faster, thereby costing less and earning more. This pattern is already emerging in Youth Training where similar controls have been introduced.

The 1992 FHE Act included safeguards to protect the interests of more vulnerable groups of learners. Yet the relative, contextual nature of many learning difficulties has made arriving at clear definitions of this group of students difficult. The FEFC has taken its responsibilities towards students with learning difficulties very seriously. Differential funding mechanisms ensure that colleges are having to address the needs of these learners at a strategic planning level. Many learning support co-ordinators are for the first time feeling a degree of empowerment although concerns are being raised about the concept of banding and individually linked funding.

REDEFINING THE FUTURE: LEARNING SUPPORT AND ACCESS COURSES

The notion of 'learning support' can include help with core skills; additional resources; modified teaching and learning methods and materials and also different modes of learning. Recently there has been a shift towards seeing provision for students with learning difficulties and disabilities as a part of 'learning support'. This is a move we welcome as it recognizes the specific needs of these students as forming part of a spectrum of learning support which any student might require at some stage of their education. In a recent FEU document *Supporting Learning – Promoting Equity and Participation,* the authors give a list of 'specific necessary variants' which certain individuals or groups might require in order to gain access to education. One of these variants is the provision of access courses. Access courses are an essential part of a college's offer in that they allow learners, who have often had an unconventional educational experience, the chance to regain their place in an educational system. Adults who chose to follow access courses could also choose to follow a conventional route to higher education – for example A levels or BTEC National/GNVQ. However, they often feel their particular learning needs require a programme of learning which will help them fill in the gaps they have missed and have the chance to receive extra support – for example through explicit teaching of a variety of study skills; through an emphasis on individual tutorials; and through having the chance to share a period of education with other students who experience difficulties similar to their own.

Our contention is that so-called 'discrete' provision for certain groups of students, particularly those with severe learning difficulties must be seen as a kind of access course. As we have already stated, these students' educational background has often been different from that of other students – they may well have attended special schools; they may have had long periods in hospital or in a long-term institution; and they may experience particular cognitive difficulties which make certain aspects of learning particularly difficult for them. We believe that certain groups of students with cognitive difficulties do have distinct needs both in content and teaching method which are at times most effectively addressed through their being taught in a distinct group. Too often the theoretical options for students with learning difficulties are seen as either provision which is totally segregated or that which is totally integrated. We maintain that what needs to be addressed is not a polarized integration/segregation debate but the specific needs of students with cognitive disabilities and what is the most effective practice which will lead to them experiencing an enhanced quality of life.

IDENTITY AND LEARNING DIFFICULTIES

We wish to focus on the right of particular groups of individuals to choose to have times when they can identify as a distinct group. To do this we wish to look very briefly at certain parallel experiences in the women's movement. In the early days of the women's movement there was often a pressure for women to prove themselves by gaining acceptance and status within a male-dominated world. It is only as the movement developed that many women began to articulate that this was not necessarily the kind of success they actually wanted to see as, on its own, it often resulted in a denial of what they felt was important to their identity as a woman. Instead they began to challenge the assumptions and values which underpin that world. In order to do this many women have felt the need to have certain times when they chose to strengthen and confirm the reality of their own beliefs in a discrete group.

Our belief is that a model in which total inclusion is seen as the only way forward can deny the specific identity, and hence undermine the dignity of people with learning difficulties and disabilities. Much has been stated about the importance of people with learning difficulties having the right to choose to integrate into the mainstream. This is a choice we would strongly advocate. However, less is articulated about the right of people to choose to spend time and receive education with a peer group of people with similar educational needs as themselves. We find that the model of integration currently formulated adheres to an individual philosophy which denies the option to spend time and sometimes to learn, within a peer group environment.

AN EXAMPLE FROM DENMARK

We wish to conclude by looking at an example of a recent research project in Denmark – *Co-write Your Own Life: Quality of Life as Discussed in the Danish Context* by Per Holm, Jesper Holst and Birger Perlt [unpublished]. In a section of their paper entitled 'The tyranny of the normal', the authors speak of 'the real danger of falling into a natural fallacy' in which a perceived notion of 'what a normal life ought to be for a particular section of the population becomes what is right for them'. Instead they feel that what is needed is 'a discussion not so much about what is normal, but about quality of life … what determines the quality of life, and what conditions are necessary to enable people to follow their own convictions and shape their own lives.' They question 'whether it is right to integrate people with learning difficulties formally into local communities without providing them with meeting or activity centres' and state how 'such places can take the form of cafes, meeting rooms, or cultural arrangements where people with learning difficulties can be together on their own terms and develop patterns of mutual interaction where they feel they are both necessary and important to each other'.

Their work with people with learning difficulties is characterized by a recognition of the primary importance of personal history and identity. From this starting point, individuals are encouraged to articulate their own vision of their future and are supported in moving towards it. Their research led them to question the validity of a product orientated approach for people with learning difficulties and also to challenge the automatic assumption of paid employment as a necessary measure of identity and self-respect. Instead they recognized the need for process-based, creative activities which would 'create real and coherent forms of co-operation and the stimulation of people with learning difficulties to form their own activities and seek new challenges'. Sometimes the skills learnt through these activities did lead on to employment activities – for example in the case where a group of people with learning difficulties took over the running of a youth hostel which was threatened with closure. Their own centre was not only 'a place where they could come together, establish social contacts and build up a sub-culture in their own terms' but also a place which other people who wanted to use the facilities could attend 'in other words, a community centre was established along untraditional lines'. Hence people with learning difficulties were seen as being an integral part of the community and as having their own essential contribution to make to it.

We believe that this model has much to teach further and adult education in the UK. Its focus moves us away from a rigid dichotomy between integration and segregation towards a model which allows for 'grouping and re-grouping'. In this model, certain parts of the curriculum offer would allow students with learning difficulties to develop their own identity and express their own aims at the same time as developing the communication and self-advocacy skills necessary to articulate these aims. There would be other times when individuals might well choose to integrate into other vocational options and learn alongside other students. Aspects of their programme would be accredited. Finally, this integration would not be seen as a 'one-way traffic' as there would be other times, in common with the Danish example, when other students could opt to take part in certain classes which were specifically focused on students with learning difficulties.

We wish to end with two riders. The first is to stress that in this paper our main concern has been with provision for those students who have a distinct cognitive disability. We have not been writing here about students with sensory or physical disabilities or about the large numbers of students whose difficulty with learning has been created by social and educational factors. Secondly, we recognize that educational provision must conform to certain standards if it is to be effective for its students. Too often the excuse has been used that, because it is difficult to arrive at suitable performance indicators, it therefore somehow can escape any kind of evaluation. One is left either with a situation in which students are made to follow unsuitable provision because it can be evaluated, or one in which they follow a programme which has no quality standards and evaluation. We maintain it is possible to evaluate and bring quality to the kind of flexible programme we have outlined, and it is here that resources and energy need to be put.

Source: MAUDSLAY, E. and DEE, L. (1995) 'Beyond the inclusionist debate' in MAUDSLAY, E. and DEE, L. (eds) *Redefining the Future: perspectives on students with learning difficulties and disabilities in further education*, London, Institute of Education, University of London, pp. 79–87.

REFERENCES

BARBER, M. (1994) *Young people and their Attitudes to School*, Keele, Keele University

BRADLEY, J. (ed.) (1985) *From Coping to Confidence*, London, FEU/NFER/DES.

BYNNER, J. and STEEDMAN, J. (1995) *Difficulties with Basic Skills: findings from the 1970 British Cohort Study, a summary*, London, Basic Skills Agency.

CERI (1986) *Disabled Youth: the right to adult status*, Paris, OECD.

CHAPPEL, A. (1992) 'Towards a sociological critique of the normalization process', *Disability and Handicap*, 7(1).

CORBETT, J. (1991) *Reflections on Training Programmes by Trainees*, London, FEU, unpublished report.

CUSACK, S. (1996) *Widening Access to Higher Education*, Bristol, HEFC.

DEARING, R. (1996) *Review of Qualifications for 16 to 19 Year Olds*, Hayes, SCAA.

DEE, L. (1988) *New Directions*, London, FEU/NFER.

DEPARTMENT FOR EDUCATION (DFE) (1994) *Code of Practice on the Identification and Assessment of Special Educational Needs*, London, DfE.

DEPARTMENT FOR EDUCATION AND EMPLOYMENT (DFEE) (1996a) *Competitiveness: creating the enterprise centre of Europe*, London, HMSO (White Paper, Cm 3300).

DEPARTMENT FOR EDUCATION AND EMPLOYMENT (DFEE) (1996b) *Funding 16–19 Education and Training: towards convergence*, London, DfEE.

DEPARTMENT FOR EDUCATION AND EMPLOYMENT (DFEE) (1996c) *Learning to Compete: education and training for 14–19 year olds*, London, DfEE.

FURTHER EDUCATION FUNDING COUNCIL (FEFC) (1995) *Funding Learning 1995/96*, London, FEFC Publications.

FURTHER EDUCATION FUNDING COUNCIL (FEFC) (1996) *Inclusive Learning*, London, FEFC Publications.

FURTHER EDUCATION UNIT (FEU) (1989) *Towards a Framework for Curriculum Entitlement*, London, FEU.

GREAT BRITAIN, PRIME MINISTER, COMMITTEE ON HIGHER EDUCATION (1963) *Higher Education: Report of the Committee appointed by the Prime Minister under the Chairmanship of Lord Robbins 1961–3*, London, HMSO (Cmnd. 2154) (the Robbins Report).

INGSTAD, B. and WHYTE, S. R. (eds) (1995) *Disability and Culture*, Berkeley, University of California Press.

MACFARLANE, E. (1993) *Education 16–19: in transition*, London, Routledge.

MAUDSLAY, E. and DEE, L. (1995) 'Beyond the inclusionist debate' in MAUDSLAY, E. and DEE, L. (eds) *Redefining the Future: perspectives on students with learning difficulties and disabilities in further education*, London, Institute of Education, University of London.

MCGINTY, J. and FISH, J. (1992) *Learning Support for Young People in Transition*, Milton Keynes, Open University Press.

MORRIS, J. (1993) *Pride Against Prejudice, transforming attitudes to disability*, London, The Women's Press Ltd.

NATIONAL UNION OF TEACHERS (NUT) (1990) *Special Education and Post-16 Students*, London, NUT.

PHILLIPS, M. (1991) 'Bigger holes means net loss', *Guardian,* 19 April 1991.

SKILL (NATIONAL BUREAU FOR STUDENTS WITH DISABILITIES) (1996) *Student Voices*, London, Skill.

TIGHT, M. (1995) *Higher Education: a part-time perspective*, Milton Keynes, Open University Press.

WARD, K., RIDDELL, S., DYER, M. and THOMSON, G. D. B. (1991) *The Transition to Adulthood of Young People with Recorded Special Educational Needs*, University of Edinburgh.

WARD, K., THOMSON, G. D. B. and RIDDELL, S. (1994) 'Transition, adulthood and special educational needs: an unresolved paradox', *European Journal of Special Needs Education,* **9**(2).

WHITTAKER, J. (1995) 'Does your college of further education have learning difficulties?' in MAUDSLAY, E. and DEE, L. (eds) *Redefining the Future: perspectives on students with learning difficulties and disabilities in further education*, London, Institute of Education, University of London.

ACKNOWLEDGEMENTS

Grateful acknowledgement is made to the following for permission to reproduce material in this unit:

Appendix 1: Department for Education (1994) *Code of Practice on the Identification and Assessment of Special Educational Needs*, © Crown copyright, reproduced with the permission of the Controller of Her Majesty's Stationery Office; *Appendix 3*: Maudslay, L. and Dee, L. (1995) *Redefining the Future: perspectives on students with learning difficulties and disabilities in further education*, Institute of Eduction, University of London.

For Appendix 2, material for the first case study was provided by Margaret Kingsford, learning support manager for Blackburn College and for the second by Jenny Wilson, the course tutor of the Team Enterprise Project at Lewisham College.